PALEO SOUPS & STEWS

over 100 delectable recipes for every season, course, and occasion

Simone Miller

VICTORY BELT PUBLISHING INC.

Las Vegas

First Published in 2016 by Victory Belt Publishing Inc.

ISBN-13: 978-1-628601-07-7

Book design by Yordan Terziev and Boryana Yordanova

Author photo and photos on pages 9, 10, 13 by Marisa Pfenning

Printed in Canada

TC0116

To the woman whose chicken soup will not be rivaled, and who loves more fiercely than anyone I know. This one's for you, Mom. Thanks for always listening to my stories.

CONTENTS

FOREWORD

To understand why I think Simone is a best-quality human, you have to know something about me first: I'm a serious introvert.

Back in 2011, I attended the Paleo f(x) conference in Austin, Texas, for the first time. I was a new cookbook author, and I was both delighted and overwhelmed to find myself in a room full of Paleo practitioners. Everyone was there! The researchers, the lifestyle gurus, the ripped fitness geeks, the bloggers . . . and me.

So there I stood, trying to figure out how to mingle—is there anything worse for introverts than mingling?!—when I found myself talking with Simone. I'm not sure if we were introduced by mutual friends or if we spontaneously started to chat, but I was smitten with her immediately. She's funny and kind, with plenty of backbone, a quick laugh, and a generous spirit.

Those are all characteristics you'll find familiar if you've cooked any of the wonderful recipes to be found on her Zenbelly blog or in her previous cookbooks. Her food and writing authentically capture who she is in real life—an irresistible blend of sophistication, earthiness, and enthusiasm for food, life, and food-life.

Simone earned her experience in the trenches of restaurant kitchens and has the chef's coat and sailor-esque vocabulary to prove it. Her recipes demonstrate a deep understanding of how flavors work together, honed by creating dishes in demanding restaurant kitchens. But she never forgets the needs of people like us: she clearly explains technique and makes high-end Paleo recipes manageable for everyone. By following her clear, supportive instructions, you will create food that looks and tastes like it came from a high-end kitchen (chef's coat and swearing optional).

In her first book, *The Zenbelly Cookbook,* Simone gave us the first truly high-end Paleo recipe collection, proving that quality ingredients will always deliver first-class flavor. With *The New Yiddish Kitchen,* she and her co-author, Jennifer Robins, invited us into their bubbes' kitchens—and put bagels, cream cheese, and kugel back on the menu.

I think we can all agree that the only thing more comforting than a bagel with a schmear is a bubbling pot of soup. But you will probably also concur that rich, hearty, velvety, sippable potions and stews are rare in the Paleo world. The ingredients traditionally used to produce those silky textures—namely heavy cream and flour—are verboten for most of us following the Paleo template. Let's also pause for a moment to mourn the loss of the go-alongs that can make soup something special: crusty bread for dipping, tender noodles for slurping, and crackers and croutons for a crunchy contrast.

Enter Simone's experience and creativity.

She's cracked the code on inventive ways to make hearty and silky soups that honor the nutrient density of the Paleo framework. And her breadsticks, crackers, noodles, and cashew yogurt? They're not "good for Paleo"; they're just good. Or, to be more accurate: Good, with a capital G.

Simone's recipes set the bar for Paleo cookbook authors, and she continues to demonstrate that the "restrictions" of Paleo aren't limitations at all. They're a call to be creative, to embrace the inherent joy in food, and to nourish ourselves with the bold flavors of quality ingredients.

I'm grateful I met Simone in that crowded room, and I'm filled with affection for her and her recipes. I wish we saw each other more often, but when I cook her food, it's like a lovely visit with her, just hanging in the kitchen. Her presence on the page is as comforting as a bowl of her luxurious Chicken and Dumplings Soup, and just as welcome.

—Melissa Joulwan

Melissa Joulwan is the author of the bestselling *Well Fed* cookbook series and the blog www.MelJoulwan.com, where she writes about her triumphs and failures in the gym, in the kitchen, and in life. Her latest cookbook is *Well Fed Weeknights: Complete Paleo Meals in 45 Minutes or Less* (November 2016).

INTRODUCTION

Is there anything more comforting than a big bowl of hearty soup or stick-to-your-ribs stew? I'm going to go out on a limb and say no. Soup is the universal love language. It can be everything from the simplest broth that you sip out of a mug to the sublime melding of flavors that you experience at the finest restaurants. It can be a hearty meal or a light lunch. It can be hot. It can be cold. It might even be sweet. It can be a velvety puree or a rustic stew. Making soup is the ultimate practice in taking a handful of ingredients and combining the flavors in just the right way to create the perfect finish. To me, that's what cooking—what *creating*—is all about. Presenting someone with a bowl of lovingly prepared soup is perhaps one of the nicest things you can do for that person.

Soup-making was part of my professional cooking life from the start. I got my first restaurant job at the age of nineteen, in a sweet little mom-and-pop vegetarian café, where I was the opener—in charge of making the coffee and the muffins and starting the soup of the day, which was always vegan. The owners had spent years developing a thick book of soup recipes. Cooking from those pages taught me a whole lot—about building flavors, using different techniques, and achieving balance. After all, making vegan soup taste incredible is a challenge because you don't have the backbone of flavor that you get from using stock. If you can make vegan soup taste incredible, you can make stock-based soup taste *really* incredible.

My second job as a soup lady was similar—at another vegetarian restaurant—but there was one glaring difference: there were no recipes to follow. *Gulp.* When I started the job, I had a moment of panic before I realized that I didn't, in fact, *need* a book full of recipes to make soup. I might have lacked confidence at that point, but I did have the experience and skill to make excellent soup.

This particular restaurant was well loved in the community, but it was poorly run. The restaurant had no real management in place, so what I would find in the walk-in each day was always a surprise. Can you guess which skill I developed while working there? You got it—the invaluable skill of improvising by taking a bunch of random ingredients and turning them into soup. I got plenty of practice with unscripted cooking while working at that disorganized café.

Years later, I got a job as a sous chef at an upscale bistro in upstate New York. The owner and head chef was thrilled that I had the chops to be in charge of the daily soup, and I was excited to have the freedom to order a huge variety of quality ingredients to make them with. I agonized over which soup I should make on my first shift, first impressions being important and all. I decided on tortilla soup, a recipe that I had made countless times; I felt that this soup was truly my best work and represented my signature style of bold but balanced flavors. I was nervous for Chef to take the first sip. I was less nervous after she took her twelfth. My soup had passed the test.

Although I'm no longer in the restaurant scene, I still make versions of the soups that I learned to make at that first restaurant job. Now I run a Paleo catering and private chef company called Zenbelly. Soups and stews are often on the menu, both for weekly clients and for special events. And tortilla soup is still a favorite among my clients.

When writing this book, I attempted to take the years of varied experience that I have making soups and stews and translate them into an easy-to-use guide. If I have done my job well, you'll learn something that I learned early on in my cooking journey: once you understand the basic formula, you can make just about any soup. You already know how to make a great tomato soup? That knowledge easily translates to making broccoli soup, believe it or not. When you have a grasp of the formula, all you need is a good pot, a handful of quality ingredients, and a little inspiration. Happy cooking!

PALEO BASICS

The Paleo way of eating has been around for several years now, and in that time, a lot has changed. When I say "the Paleo way of eating," I'm referring to the *modern* Paleo way of eating, not the actual Paleolithic way of eating (which obviously dates back more than a few years). A lot of people assume that these two things are one and the same, but they are actually quite different.

DOESN'T PALEO = THE CAVEMAN DIET?

A lot of people think that eating Paleo means eating like a caveperson—consuming nuts, raw vegetables and fruits, and lots of meat—but that is an extremely oversimplified way of looking at it. Although Paleo is based on a pre-agricultural diet, the foods that our cave-dwelling ancestors ate and the foods that we eat today as part of a Paleo lifestyle don't have much of a resemblance. Today's Paleo diet is not meant to be a historical reenactment. Back in the Paleolithic era, people weren't shopping at mega markets or farmer's markets. They were hunting and gathering, and the plants and animals that they were eating looked very different from those that are available to us today. Sure, we can still call it Paleo, but let's get on the same page about what that means.

FIRST THINGS FIRST: CUT OUT PROCESSED FOODS

This is the *big thing* in a Paleo lifestyle! We're all busy, and convenience foods are definitely convenient. Unfortunately, though, a lot of us have fallen into the habit of relying on those foods as our main source of sustenance. Highly processed foods that contain added sugars, gums, emulsifiers, and artificial colors and flavors simply don't pack the same nutritional punch as fresh veggies and properly raised meats. Lists of "yes" and "no" foods are helpful when starting a Paleo way of eating, but if you follow the one simple guideline of eating real, unprocessed foods, you're off to a great start.

Foods without labels—meaning that they have only one ingredient—are best: plants, animals, and healthy fats. When possible, choosing organic plants and animals that were raised properly is ideal. Grains and legumes are not part of the Paleo template, but some people reintroduce them after a cleansing or healing period and find that they can tolerate them quite well. Following a Paleo lifestyle is really about finding what works for you; there's no one way of eating that works for everyone.

MORE SPECIFICALLY, EAT THESE FOODS

Meat, seafood, and eggs: Beef, pork, lamb, chicken, turkey, eggs, fish, and shellfish are all great sources of protein. If it's available and affordable, meat from animals that were raised properly rather than on factory farms is best. Here's the good news about this book: the cuts of meat used to make soups and stews are often among the least expensive cuts.

Plants and fungi (vegetables, fruits, and mushrooms): Leafy, cruciferous, and starchy veggies, both fresh and frozen, and fruits of all kinds are great sources of micronutrients and good carbohydrates. If you are able to purchase organic, seasonal, and local produce, that's even better.

Healthy fats: After decades of being wrongfully vilified, fats are finally getting the recognition they deserve as a vital part of a healthy diet. Animal fats such as lard, tallow, and duck fat are great for cooking because they don't degrade when heated to high temperatures. Purchase high-quality animal fats whenever possible; they're often available at natural foods stores, gourmet markets, and online.

Although some people who eat Paleo exclude all dairy, many people find that they tolerate ghee quite well. This is because the milk solids have been removed, leaving only the butterfat and making ghee much easier to digest than butter. Ghee's high smoke point and rich, nutty flavor make it great for cooking.

Avocado oil is another good option for high-heat cooking. Extra-virgin olive oil is best used cold for finishing soups and using in sauces. Industrial seed and "vegetable" oils—such as soy, corn, and canola oils—are best avoided because they are highly processed and often rancid.

Nuts and seeds are another good source of healthy fats. They are great for snacking, for garnishing dishes, and for use in condiments and baked goods.

Paleo-friendly flavor boosters: Eating Paleo does not mean that your diet will suddenly become bland and boring. In fact, most of my favorite ways to boost flavor and create balance are perfectly acceptable in a Paleo template. Ingredients in this category include fish sauce, coconut aminos, chili paste, tomato paste, citrus zest and juice, and fresh herbs. You might need to check the ingredients on some packaged items.

Specialty ingredients for baking: I designed the baked goods in this book to come as close to their grain-based counterparts as possible. It's important to me that a grain-free baguette tastes like a regular baguette. My recipes for noodles, breads, and crackers use ingredients such as finely ground blanched almond flour, cassava flour, potato starch, and arrowroot starch. I also use small amounts of some natural sweeteners, like coconut sugar and honey. Some of these ingredients may be unfamiliar to you, but you can easily find them online if you are unable to source them at your local market.

Check the Shopping Guide on page 267 for online shopping information—all of my favorite brands are listed there.

HOW THE RECIPES IN THIS BOOK
FALL INTO THE PALEO TEMPLATE

The recipes in this book are Paleo-friendly, meaning that they are made without grains, legumes, cane sugar, industrial seed and vegetable oils, and, for the most part, dairy. Are some gray-area foods included? Sure. I don't see Paleo as a strict diet but as a template that can be tweaked to fit each individual's needs. A few recipes include dairy as an option, but you can easily make them dairy-free if you prefer.

SOUP-MAKING TECHNIQUES

Soup, by definition, is about the most basic dish you can create, and it can be considered the epitome of simple peasant food. In fact, many beloved comfort food dishes are the result of someone's great-great-grandmother making a meal out of the veggie scraps and cheap cuts of meat that she had on hand. Quite often, incredible soups and stews are made just like that—by rummaging through the fridge and digging out the stockpot.

However, because this cookbook is focused on soup, you would probably like a bit more direction than that, yes? I thought so. But please do something for me while cooking from this book: don't overcomplicate things. I have tried my best to write detailed instructions so that you can get the best results possible, but the beauty of soup-making is that it is not an exact science.

That being said, making a really good soup usually involves a bit more than just boiling all the ingredients in a big pot of water. Here is a quick overview of the key techniques used in this book:

Sauté: To cook ingredients in some sort of fat until browned and softened, often over medium-high or high heat. The browning of the ingredients in fat adds depth of flavor to a soup or stew.

Sweat: To cook ingredients, often salted, in fat until they become softened but not browned. Sweating vegetables, which is often done over medium-low or medium heat, brings out some of their natural sweetness without adding the deeper flavor that sautéing creates.

Caramelize: To cook an ingredient in fat over low heat for an extended period until the ingredient is sweet, golden brown, and softened. Caramelizing an ingredient draws out its natural sugars and essentially transforms the ingredient into a whole new animal (or vegetable). If you were just dropped onto this planet and tried a piece of raw onion and then a piece of caramelized onion, you would not believe that they were the same vegetable—I guarantee it.

Sear: To cook a food (often meat) in fat over medium-high or high heat to brown the exterior and create a hard crust. The desired result when searing is called the Maillard reaction, which Merriam-Webster defines as "a nonenzymatic reaction between sugars and proteins that occurs upon heating and that produces browning of some foods (as meat and bread)." In other words, searing uses heat to brown an ingredient in order to amplify its flavor and appearance. *Note:* I've included the step of searing meat in the recipes in this book only when I feel that it makes a noticeable difference in the finished soup or stew (see "To Sear or Not to Sear," opposite).

To Sear or Not to Sear?

Before I began writing this book, my default method for cooking soup or stew always involved searing the meat being used in the recipe. That has changed. This decision didn't come easily, because the chef in me assumed that searing the meat was the first step in obtaining the best flavor and texture. However, because busy home cooks often turn to soups and stews expecting to be able to prepare a meal quickly and with few steps, I decided to test this assumption. Is the extra step of searing really necessary? My conclusion: sometimes, but not always. In many recipes, I do not notice a big difference between searing the meat before adding it to the soup or stew and simply adding the raw meat. In some cases, I actually find that *not* searing results in more tender meat.

Because the searing step can be somewhat time-consuming and creates more cleanup work, I don't include it in any recipes that don't truly benefit from it. For example, in recipes such as Spicy Lamb Curry (page 158) and Zenbelly Chili 2.0 (page 162), where the desired result is meltingly tender meat, skipping the searing step works well. If a recipe in this book does begin with the step of searing the meat, it's because I feel that the extra step truly adds something to the dish, whether it's a deeper flavor or an enhanced texture. In my Chicken and Dumplings Soup (page 136), for example, the chicken is dredged in arrowroot starch and browned; this two-part process both flavors the chicken and thickens the soup because of the starch that browns in the pan.

Boil: To cook a mixture, usually over medium-high or high heat, so that the liquid produces lots of large bubbles and is hot enough to reduce (see below) at a pretty rapid rate. Boiling is used to get things really cooking and to reduce the liquid to concentrate the flavors.

Simmer: To cook a mixture, usually over low to medium-low heat, so that the liquid produces small bubbles. You can think of a simmer as a baby boil. Simmering cooks the mixture gently over an extended period, which allows the flavors to really develop.

Reduce: To boil a mixture so that evaporation occurs, thus concentrating the flavors. Some people consider reducing to be the most complicated technique in cooking because it's tough to know when something has sufficiently reduced. What's my solution to that difficulty? Taste it! Tasting as you go is the most important thing you can do while cooking. If your broth tastes watery, keep reducing it. If your soup seems too thin, keep reducing it. Did you reduce it too much? Don't panic—just add more water or broth. I often purposely reduce broth more than necessary so that it becomes rich and concentrated. Then I can either use it as is or dilute it with water, depending on the recipe I'm using it for.

In addition to the above techniques, you will find at the beginning of certain chapters more detailed information that is specific to the recipes in that chapter, including techniques that are particularly relevant to that category of soup or stew.

A Note About Tomatoes

Because the quality of fresh tomatoes varies greatly throughout the year, the recipes in this book call for canned tomatoes. This is done both for the sake of consistency and for ease. If, however, you have access to good, fresh tomatoes, it's an easy swap to use them instead. For each 14-ounce can of tomatoes, you'll need 1 pound of fresh tomatoes. To prepare them, simply cut an X in the bottom of each tomato and place them in a large bowl. Pour boiling water over the tomatoes, cover, and let sit for 5 to 10 minutes, until the skins start to loosen. Pour off the hot water and run cold water over them. Once they're cool enough to handle, peel and cut out the core of each tomato. Gently squeeze out the seeds and dice the tomatoes, catching as much of the juices as possible. If the recipe calls for pureeing the soup (or you'd prefer fewer tomato chunks in the end product), you can also crush the tomatoes into a bowl using your hands.

SEASONING TO TASTE

Let's talk some more about tasting, because I think it's especially important when it comes to soups and stews. If you own my first cookbook, *The Zenbelly Cookbook*, you may have noticed that I do not say, "Add salt to taste." There's a reason for that: how can you be expected to know what something you've never had is supposed to taste like? In that book I tried to be very specific with measurements of salt, pepper, and other seasonings so that the finished dish that you make is as close as possible to what I make.

With soups and stews, though, seasoning is a bit different because there are more factors at play than with, say, pan-roasted chicken with bacon and apples or coffee-rubbed flat-iron fajitas. (Two dishes that you could have in your life if you owned *The Zenbelly Cookbook*—see what I did there?)

THE FACTORS THAT AFFECT SEASONING

· **The saltiness and richness of the broth that you use:** This is the main factor. Some broths are very light-tasting and don't add much more flavor than water. Others fall on the opposite end of the spectrum and have a robust flavor. For this reason, I recommend using a light hand with salt until the soup or stew is almost done. Tasting when the soup is nearly done cooking is a good way to make sure that you don't use too much salt or over-season.

· **The variation in size of your vegetables:** Mother Nature doesn't create every carrot in exactly the same size, and they're not all uniform in the grocery store, either. Sometimes I include descriptions of sizes, such as "small" or "large," and weights in the ingredient lists, but let's be honest: most people aren't going to weigh their carrots before chopping them—which is fine. Inherently imprecise and subjective descriptors such as "small" and "large" do not guarantee the exact same results, either: what I think of as "large" may not be exactly the same as what you think of as "large." Tasting as you go will allow you to adjust for these size differences.

· **The flavor of your ingredients:** Wait, what? Doesn't celery always taste the same? Well, somewhat, but there's a range in flavor. The same can be said of onions. If you are mincing one onion for shepherd's pie, it won't make that much of a difference whether the onion is on the sweeter or the spicier side, but when the majority of the flavor of a broth, soup, or stew is coming from the vegetables infused into it, the sweetness or spiciness of that onion can have a big impact.

· **The finishes and condiments:** Some soups get a lot of flavor from ingredients that are added at the very end, such as fresh herbs or citrus juice, or from a condiment that's added to each bowl. For example, if the last step in a recipe recommends adding something salty, such as pesto (see my recipe on page 206), the ingredient list for the soup might include only a small amount of salt so that the end result isn't too salty. You'll find a wide variety of soup garnishes in Chapter 7 of this book.

You'll notice that in the last step of a recipe I often instruct you to season to taste with salt and/or other seasonings. Know that this is always an as-needed step; if you taste the soup and it's perfect, great! You're done—break out the ladle. If the flavor falls a bit flat, however, you may need to add more salt, spice, citrus juice, or whatever else is recommended for the recipe.

COOKING TERMS

Chop: To cut a food into rough pieces, often for use in a broth or a soup that is going to be pureed.

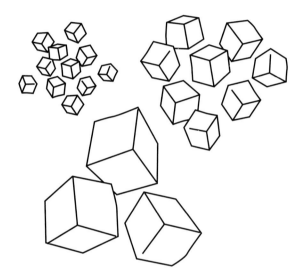

Julienne: To cut a food into long, skinny strips or matchsticks, about 2 inches long and as thin as possible.

Dice: To cut a food into cubes. Small dice are about 1/4 inch; medium dice are about 1/2 inch; and large dice are about 1 inch. If a recipe calls for an ingredient to be simply "diced," it means medium dice.

Mince: To chop a food as finely as you can with a knife. You can also use a Microplane grater or food processor for this task. Garlic is often minced.

Divided: If an ingredient is used more than once in a recipe, the word *divided* will appear after that ingredient in the ingredient list. This term often applies to oil and salt, when food is cooked in batches or salted throughout the cooking process. *Divided* is a heads-up not to throw in the total amount of that ingredient the first time you see it in the instructions.

TOOLS AND EQUIPMENT

Want to know the good news about making soup? Here it is: you probably already have all of the tools and equipment you'll need to whip up a batch.

COOKWARE

Stockpot: An 8- to 10-quart stainless-steel stockpot is indispensable for making large batches of broth and soup.

Heavy-bottomed pot: A good-quality stainless-steel or cast-iron pot is your best friend when it comes to making soups and stews. I use my 7¼-quart enameled cast-iron Dutch oven for every pot of soup that I make, as well as for countless other recipes.

Slow cooker (6- to 8-quart capacity):
If your schedule does not allow for starting to cook dinner an hour or more before mealtime, a slow cooker is an excellent appliance for you to have. Dinner can cook while you're at work or while you're sleeping.

Multi-cooker (6- to 8-quart capacity):
This multitasking workhorse does practically everything: slow-cook, pressure-cook, sauté, and steam. Some multi-cookers also have a yogurt setting, which is useful for making dairy-free yogurt and other cultured foods. If you are in need of either a pressure cooker or a slow cooker, I recommend getting a multi-cooker instead.

Pressure cooker (6- to 8-quart capacity, or larger if a stovetop variety):
I promise that using a pressure cooker isn't scary. Today's pressure cookers have safety features that prevent kitchen explosions, and they're an excellent way to drastically cut cooking time. For example, a beef stew that would normally cook for 2 or more hours on the stovetop can be prepared in a pressure cooker in about 35 minutes.

There are two pressure cooker options available: stovetop and electric. I prefer a large (8- to 10-quart) stovetop version for making large batches of broth, but I love using an electric pressure cooker for soups and stews because it's easier to control the pressure and cooking time. Of course, you can use an electric model for making broth; you will just have a smaller yield. Often this is not a problem because the broth is more concentrated and can be thinned with water for use in recipes.

OTHER ITEMS

Rimmed baking sheets: For roasting meats and veggies. I also use rimmed baking sheets for quite a few of the baked goods in this book.

Large colander: For draining noodles and rinsing veggies.

Fine-mesh strainer: For straining broth.

Blender: A standard jar blender yields smooth purees and is the best tool to use for the blended soups in this book (see Chapter 3).

Immersion blender: An immersion blender (sometimes called a stick blender) produces coarser pureed soup, but the advantage of using one is that you can blend the soup right in the cooking pot. It is possible to get a relatively smooth puree with an immersion blender, but it takes some time.

Food processor: For blending coarse purees and pestos and quickly rough-chopping vegetables.

Wooden spoons and spatulas: For mixing it all up (and sneaking a taste).

Julienne peeler or spiral slicer: For making veggie noodles of all kinds (see page 194 for my recipe). A spiral slicer is a handy tool that's designed specifically for this task, but a simple and inexpensive julienne peeler (pictured) will get the job done, too.

Slotted spoon: For removing solids from soup, specifically aromatics that have done their job once they've infused into the broth.

Food thermometer: For checking the internal temperature of meats to ensure that they are fully cooked and safe to eat, and for checking that soups are cool enough to store safely (see the sidebar below).

Glass jars and other containers: Soups and stews make the ultimate leftovers. One-quart glass jars are great for storing broth (if you're freezing it, use freezer-safe jars and fill them three-quarters of the way full so they don't explode when the liquid freezes and expands), and larger glass containers are perfect for storing soup that doesn't get eaten right away.

Cooling and Storing Broths, Soups, and Stews

Foods such as soups and stews that take a long time to cool are more likely to cause food-borne illness, so it's important to cool and store them quickly to minimize this risk.

The goal of the following methods is to minimize the time the food spends in the temperature "danger zone" of 41°F to 135°F. This temperature range is quite hospitable to bacteria, so we want our food to spend as little time in it as possible.

To quickly bring hot broth, soup, or stew to a safe temperature:

- If a broth or soup tastes more concentrated than necessary, you can use ice cubes to dilute and cool it.

- Make an ice bath in a clean sink or large container. Place the vessel containing the broth, soup, or stew in the ice bath and stir frequently to disperse the heat.

- Transfer the soup to multiple large, shallow metal containers and place them uncovered in the fridge, stirring often to disperse the heat. If using this method, don't fill the containers much more than a couple of inches. This method is best done after you have already cooled the soup a bit so that you don't overtax your fridge or warm the other foods in it.

Once the soup is cool (below 41°F), you can transfer it to your preferred storage containers. If using glass containers for freezing, be sure to use freezer-safe containers and fill them only three-quarters full to allow for expansion.

HOW TO USE THIS BOOK

For easy reference, the chapters in this book are organized by recipe type: broths and basics, chilled soups, hearty soups, and so on. You'll also find chapters containing recipes that are meant to be mixed and matched with the soup recipes: Chapter 6, "In the Bowl," contains noodles and other fun additions; Chapter 7, "On Top," contains garnishes to add the perfect pop of flavor; and Chapter 8, "On the Side," contains breads, crackers, and dippers. Within the recipes, you'll see suggestions for recipe pairings. And of course, you should feel free to play with your own combinations if you're inspired to do so.

ALTERNATIVE COOKING METHODS

Because of the growing popularity of slow cookers, pressure cookers, and multi-cookers, I've included multiple cooking methods for many of the recipes in this book. Stovetop cooking instructions are presented first as the default method for all of the recipes; they're followed by alternatives for using a slow cooker or pressure cooker. If a recipe does not have instructions for using an alternative cooking method, it's because you won't save any time or energy by using the special equipment.

When a recipe does include slow cooker and/or pressure cooker instructions, you'll see their cook time(s) at the top of the recipe. The slow cooker and pressure cooker methods are marked with these icons:

 **SLOW COOKER**    **PRESSURE COOKER**

QUICK RECIPES

Soup is one of those wonderful dishes that can often be whipped up in no time, so you'll find lots of recipes in this book that can be prepared, from start to finish, in one hour or less. Note that the timing is based on the stovetop method and includes prep work and cooking and/or chilling. For recipes that can be made in a pressure cooker, the start-to-finish time is reduced considerably.

SPECIAL DIETS

If you have food restrictions that go beyond Paleo, see the Special Diets section (page 272) for easy reference of recipes that are Autoimmune Protocol compliant, lower-carb, egg-free, and nut-free.

CHAPTER 1:

BROTHS AND BASICS

Good broth will resurrect the dead.
—South American proverb

One of the first life lessons that I learned as a kid is that the sniffles equal chicken soup. I'm pretty sure there was never a time when my brother or I felt a tickle in our throats that we were not presented with a bowl of piping-hot chicken soup within hours. It was like a reflex for my mother. As a kid, I just assumed that it was what all Jewish mothers did. (Chicken soup is known as "Jewish penicillin," after all.) Now, as an adult with a little bit of nutrition education under my belt, I know that soup brings more than comfort when we're feeling under the weather.

There's actual science behind the theory that chicken soup is good for you. Broths and stocks have true health benefits, and they've been used as a healing remedy by nearly every culture. They contain nutrients such as calcium, magnesium, phosphorus, and trace minerals in a form that is easily absorbed by the body. They also contain materials such as chondroitin sulfates and glucosamine, which are broken down from the cartilage and tendons used in the broth and are commonly recommended for joint and bone health. In addition, the gelatin and collagen in properly made bone broth are excellent for skin, hair, and nail health.

BROTH, STOCK, AND BONE BROTH: WHAT'S THE DIFFERENCE?

Technically, broth, stock, and bone broth are quite similar; the difference is in the details.

- **Broth** is made from meat, vegetables, and aromatics that are simmered in water and seasoned. Broth can include some bones, but by definition it does not need them. A broth typically needs to cook for only 45 minutes to 2 hours in order to pull the flavor out of the ingredients. The main purpose of broth is to add flavor to soups and sauces. It is also sipped on its own as a light soup.

- **Stock** is made from bones (often with some meat and fat still on them), vegetables, and aromatics that are simmered in water for a longer period than broth—often more than 4 hours. The purpose of making stock is to pull the collagen from the bones, which gives the stock a rich, gelatinous consistency. Stock is typically not seasoned so that it remains neutral for the recipes to which it's added.

- **Bone broth** is essentially the same as stock, but it's often cooked for an even longer time to extract as many minerals from the bones as possible. It is also often seasoned and sipped on its own, making it something of a hybrid of stock and broth. Traditionally, vinegar is added at the beginning of the process to help extract the minerals from the bones.

Store-bought broths and stocks are widely available and vary greatly in quality. For the most part, the conventional varieties are called broth or stock without much difference in how they're made. Their purpose is to flavor soups and sauces, and they don't have the same nutritional benefits as homemade broth. Store-bought broths and stocks also often include undesirable ingredients, such as MSG, sugar, mystery "natural" flavors, and massive amounts of sodium.

Bone broth companies are popping up all over in response to the growing popularity of this magic elixir. For the most part, these companies make their bone broth the traditional way, using quality ingredients. Purchasing bone broth from a reputable company is a great time-saving alternative to making your own at home. Many bone broth companies ship nationwide, but it may be more cost-effective to find a company near where you live, if possible.

The broth recipes in this chapter will give you a good foundation for all of the soup recipes that follow. In a perfect world, with 72 hours in each day and a full-time dishwasher, I would always make my own broth. But since writing this cookbook required a lot of broth for all of the soup I was making, I used bone broth from Osso Good Bones, a company that is local to me in the San Francisco Bay Area. They lovingly make exceptional broth that is great for both sipping and using as a base for soup. (See the Shopping Guide on page 267 for more information.)

The recipes in this chapter were developed with the intention of drawing as much flavor out of the ingredients as possible. This sometimes means that they involve a few extra steps, but you shouldn't find any of them to be difficult or complicated. All of the broths in this book were intended to be used in the soup and stew chapters that follow, but they are all delicious enough to pour into a mug and sip on their own.

REGARDING COOKING TIMES

The recipes in this chapter were created from a culinary standpoint and with practicality in mind, so you won't see cook times of 12 or more hours as you might in many ancestral and Paleo recipes. If your intention is to draw as much gelatin out of the bones as possible, you can simmer the bones for much longer, up to 12 hours on the stovetop or for days in a slow cooker. If that simply isn't practical for you and you still want more gelatin in your diet, you can add gelatin to any of the broths or soups in this book. See the Shopping Guide on page 267 for more information. All that being said, when I make bone broth using the methods and cook times outlined in this chapter, I wind up with extremely gelatinous broth.

ROASTED VEGETABLE BROTH

YIELD: 2 quarts | PREP TIME: 15 minutes
STOVETOP: about 2 hours | SLOW COOKER: 7 to 9 hours | PRESSURE COOKER: about 1 hour 30 minutes

3/4 pound celery root (about 1 small), peeled and trimmed

1/2 pound celery (about 1/2 bunch)

1 large onion

3/4 pound carrots (about 4 large)

3/4 pound parsnips (about 2 medium), peeled

1 pound golden beets (about 2 large)

1 bulb garlic, broken into cloves and unpeeled

1 pound cremini mushrooms (about 15 large)

1/4 cup avocado oil or other high-heat cooking fat (see page 16)

1 cup white wine, or 1/4 cup white wine vinegar mixed with 3/4 cup water

6 sprigs fresh parsley

1 sprig fresh rosemary

1 teaspoon salt

10 to 12 black peppercorns

AIP Modification: *Omit the peppercorns.*

01 Preheat the oven to 450°F.

02 Dice the vegetables into roughly 1-inch chunks. Leave the garlic cloves and mushrooms whole. In a large bowl, toss the vegetables with the oil. Spread the veggies on two rimmed baking sheets.

03 Roast the vegetables for 30 minutes. Give them a stir and return the baking sheets to the oven, rotating the pans if they're not cooking evenly. Roast for another 30 to 45 minutes, until the veggies are well roasted and browned. Transfer the vegetables to a large pot.

04 Pour 1/2 cup of the white wine onto each baking sheet and scrape up any browned bits that are stuck to the pan.

05 Pour the liquid from the baking sheets over the vegetables in the pot and cover with 3 quarts (12 cups) of cool water. Add the parsley, rosemary, salt, and peppercorns and bring to a boil over high heat. Turn the heat down to medium until the broth is at a low boil. Continue cooking at a low boil for 45 minutes to 1 hour, until the liquid has reduced by about one-quarter.

06 Strain the broth, pressing out as much liquid from the vegetables as possible, and discard the vegetables. Store the broth in a glass jar in the refrigerator for up to 1 week or in the freezer for up to a year.

 Slow Cooker Instructions: *After completing Step 3, transfer the roasted vegetables to a slow cooker. Complete Step 4, then pour the liquid from the baking sheets into the slow cooker with the vegetables. Add the remaining ingredients and 2 quarts of cool water. Cook on low for 6 to 8 hours, until the vegetables are very soft. Strain and store the broth as described in Step 6.*

 Pressure Cooker Instructions: *After completing Step 3, transfer the roasted vegetables to a pressure cooker. Complete Step 4, then pour the liquid from the baking sheets into the pressure cooker. Add the remaining ingredients and 2 quarts of cool water. Secure the lid and cook on high pressure for 15 minutes, then allow the pressure to release naturally for 10 minutes before opening the lid. Strain and store the broth as described in Step 6.*

VEGGIE-HERB BROTH

YIELD: 2 quarts | **PREP TIME:** 15 minutes
STOVETOP: 1 hour | **SLOW COOKER:** 6 to 8 hours | **PRESSURE COOKER:** 25 minutes

½ pound carrots, chopped

½ pound parsnips, peeled and chopped

½ pound celery (about ½ bunch), chopped

2 large leeks, cleaned and chopped (see Tip)

1 small celery root, peeled and chopped

2 cloves garlic, unpeeled

1 small bunch fresh parsley

1 small bunch fresh dill

1 small bunch fresh chives

1 teaspoon salt

01 Place all of the ingredients in a large pot and cover with 3 quarts of cool water.

02 Cover and bring to a boil. Once boiling, reduce the heat to medium so it's at a low boil. Cook for 1 hour, or until the vegetables are very soft and the liquid has reduced by about one-quarter.

03 Use a fine-mesh strainer to strain the broth, pressing out as much liquid from the vegetables as possible. Store the broth in a glass jar in the refrigerator for up to 1 week or in the freezer for up to a year.

 Slow Cooker Instructions: *Place all of the ingredients in a slow cooker and cover with 2 quarts of cool water. Cook on low for 6 to 8 hours, until the vegetables are very soft and the liquid has reduced by about one-quarter. Proceed with Step 3.*

 Pressure Cooker Instructions: *Place all of the ingredients in a pressure cooker and cover with 2 quarts of cool water. Secure the lid. Cook on high pressure for 15 minutes. Allow the pressure to release naturally for 10 minutes before opening the lid. Proceed with Step 3.*

Chef's Tip: *To clean the leeks, slice them in half lengthwise and run under water, separating the layers to remove all of the dirt. Shake off the excess water.*

CHICKEN BROTH

YIELD: 2 quarts | PREP TIME: 15 minutes
STOVETOP: about 3 hours | SLOW COOKER: 8 to 10 hours | PRESSURE COOKER: about 2 hours

4 pounds chicken bones, including backs, necks, feet, and wings

2 tablespoons apple cider vinegar

2 teaspoons salt

10 to 12 black peppercorns

1 large onion, unpeeled, quartered

½ pound carrots, chopped

½ pound celery (about ½ bunch), chopped

½ pound celery root, peeled and chopped

½ pound parsnips, peeled and chopped

1 large handful fresh herbs, such as parsley, dill, or a combination

AIP Modification: *Omit the peppercorns.*

01 Place the chicken bones, vinegar, salt, and peppercorns in a large pot and cover with 3 quarts of cool water. Bring to a boil and cook, uncovered, for 10 minutes. Skim off and discard any scum that has risen to the top of the pot.

02 Reduce the heat to low and simmer, covered, for 2 hours.

03 Add the onion, carrots, celery, celery root, parsnips, and herbs. Bring to a boil and cook, uncovered, for 1 hour, or until the liquid has reduced by about one-quarter.

04 Use a fine-mesh strainer to strain the broth, pressing as much liquid from the bones and vegetables as possible before discarding them. Store the broth in a glass jar in the refrigerator for up to 1 week or in the freezer for up to a year.

 Slow Cooker Instructions: *Place all of the ingredients in a slow cooker and cover with 2 quarts of cool water. Cook on low for 8 to 10 hours, until the liquid has reduced by about one-quarter. Proceed with Step 4.*

 Pressure Cooker Instructions: *Place the bones, vinegar, salt, and peppercorns in a pressure cooker and cover with 2 quarts of cool water. Secure the lid and cook on high pressure for 1 hour. Allow the pressure to release naturally for 10 minutes before opening the lid. Add the onion, carrots, celery, celery root, parsnips, and herbs. Cook over high heat, uncovered (or use the sauté function if using a multi-cooker), and boil for 1 hour. Proceed with Step 4.*

BASIC BEEF BROTH

YIELD: 2 quarts | **PREP TIME:** 10 minutes
STOVETOP: 4 to 6 hours | **SLOW COOKER:** 10 to 12 hours | **PRESSURE COOKER:** about 2 hours

4 pounds beef bones (knuckle bones are best)

1 (2-inch) piece fresh ginger, chopped

2 tablespoons apple cider vinegar

2 teaspoons salt

10 to 12 black peppercorns

1 large onion, unpeeled and quartered

½ pound celery (about ½ bunch), chopped

6 to 8 cloves garlic, unpeeled

2 sprigs fresh herbs, such as thyme, rosemary, or savory, or a combination

AIP Modification: *Omit the peppercorns.*

01 Place the beef bones in a large pot and cover with water. Bring to a boil and cook for 3 to 5 minutes, until there is a good layer of scum at the top. Dump the entire contents of the pot into a clean sink. Rinse the bones well, scrubbing them with your hands a bit to remove any remaining scum. Set the bones aside.

02 Wash the pot.

03 Return the bones to the pot and add the ginger, vinegar, salt, peppercorns, and 3 quarts of cool water. Bring to a boil. Turn the heat down to low and simmer, partially covered, for 4 to 6 hours. Add the onion, celery, garlic, and herbs during the last hour of cooking.

04 Use a fine-mesh strainer to strain the broth, pressing as much liquid from the bones and vegetables as possible before discarding them. Store the broth in a glass jar in the refrigerator for up to 1 week or in the freezer for up to a year.

 Slow Cooker Instructions: *After completing Step 1, transfer the bones to a slow cooker and add the remaining ingredients and 2 quarts of cool water. Cook on low for 10 to 12 hours. Proceed with Step 4.*

 Pressure Cooker Instructions: *After completing Step 1, transfer the bones to a pressure cooker. Add the ginger, vinegar, salt, peppercorns, and 2 quarts of cool water. Secure the lid and cook on high pressure for 1 hour. Allow the pressure to release naturally for 10 minutes before opening the lid. Add the remaining ingredients, bring to a boil over high heat (or use the sauté function if using a multi-cooker), and boil, uncovered, for 1 hour. Proceed with Step 4.*

ROASTED BEEF AND MUSHROOM BROTH

YIELD: 2 quarts | **PREP TIME:** 5 minutes
STOVETOP: 5 to 7 hours | **SLOW COOKER:** 11 to 13 hours | **PRESSURE COOKER:** about 2 hours

4 pounds beef bones (knuckle bones are best)

1 large onion, unpeeled and quartered

1 pound whole cremini mushrooms

6 to 8 cloves garlic, unpeeled

2 tablespoons apple cider vinegar

2 teaspoons salt

10 to 12 black peppercorns

2 sprigs fresh herbs, such as thyme, rosemary, or savory, or a combination

AIP Modification: *Omit the peppercorns.*

01 Preheat the oven to 450°F.

02 Place the beef bones in a large pot and cover with 3 quarts of cool water. Bring to a boil and cook for 3 to 5 minutes, until there is a good layer of scum at the top. Dump the entire contents of the pot into a clean sink. Rinse the bones well, scrubbing them with your hands a bit to get off any remaining scum.

03 Transfer the bones to a rimmed baking sheet along with the onion, mushrooms, and garlic. Roast for 30 to 45 minutes, until the bones are golden brown.

04 Wash the pot, then transfer the contents of the baking sheet to it. Add the vinegar, salt, and peppercorns. Cover with 3 quarts of cool water and bring to a boil.

05 Partially cover the pot and turn the heat down to low. Simmer for 4 to 6 hours, adding the herbs during the last hour of cooking.

06 Use a fine-mesh strainer to strain the broth, pressing as much liquid from the bones and vegetables as possible before discarding. Store the broth in a glass jar in the refrigerator for up to 1 week or in the freezer for up to a year.

 Slow Cooker Instructions: *After completing Step 3, transfer the contents of the baking sheet to a slow cooker and add the vinegar, salt, peppercorns, and 2 quarts of cool water. Cook on low for 10 to 12 hours, adding the herbs during the last hour of cooking. Proceed with Step 6.*

 Pressure Cooker Instructions: *After completing Step 3, transfer the contents of the baking sheet to a pressure cooker and add the vinegar, salt, peppercorns, and 2 quarts of cool water. Secure the lid and cook on high pressure for 1 hour. Allow the pressure to release naturally for 10 minutes before opening the lid. Add the herbs. Cook over high heat, uncovered (or use the sauté function if using a multi-cooker), and boil for 15 minutes. Proceed with Step 6.*

PORK BROTH
with shiitake mushrooms and ginger

YIELD: 2 quarts | PREP TIME: 5 minutes
STOVETOP: about 4 hours | SLOW COOKER: about 10 to 12 hours | PRESSURE COOKER: about 1 hour

4 pounds pork bones, ideally including a foot

2 large leeks, cleaned and chopped (see Tip on page 38)

1 (4-inch) piece fresh ginger, sliced

½ ounce dried shiitake mushrooms

2 tablespoons apple cider vinegar

2 teaspoons salt

10 to 12 black peppercorns

AIP Modification: *Omit the peppercorns.*

01 Place the pork bones in a large pot and cover with water. Bring to a boil and cook for 3 to 5 minutes, until there is a good layer of scum at the top. Dump the entire contents of the pot into a clean sink. Rinse the bones well, scrubbing them with your hands to remove any remaining scum. Set the bones aside.

02 Clean the pot.

03 Return the bones to the pot and add the leeks, ginger, mushrooms, vinegar, salt, peppercorns, and 10 cups of cool water.

04 Partially cover the pot and bring the contents to a boil. Turn the heat down to a strong simmer and cook for 4 hours.

05 Use a fine-mesh strainer to strain the broth, pressing as much liquid from the bones and vegetables as possible before discarding them. Store the broth in a glass jar in the refrigerator for up to 1 week or in the freezer for up to a year.

 Slow Cooker Instructions: *After completing Step 1, transfer the bones to a slow cooker. Add the remaining ingredients and 2 quarts of cool water. Cook on low for 10 to 12 hours. Proceed with Step 5.*

 Pressure Cooker Instructions: *After completing Step 1, transfer the bones to a pressure cooker. Add the remaining ingredients and 7 cups of cool water. Secure the lid and cook on high pressure for 1 hour, then allow the pressure to release naturally for 10 minutes before opening the lid. Proceed with Step 5.*

DASHI BROTH

 YIELD: 2 quarts | **PREP TIME:** 30 minutes | **STOVETOP:** 20 to 30 minutes

2 (4-inch square) pieces kombu

1 cup (1 ounce) bonito flakes

1 small bunch chives or garlic chives (optional)

01 Place the kombu in a large pot and cover with 2 quarts of cool water. Allow to soak for 30 minutes.

02 Place the pot over high heat and bring to a boil, then lower the heat to a simmer. Simmer for 10 to 15 minutes, then add the bonito flakes and chives, if using, and turn off the heat. Let steep for 10 to 15 minutes, until the bonito sinks to the bottom of the pot.

03 Strain the broth through a fine-mesh strainer lined with cheesecloth to catch any sediment. Store the broth in a glass jar in the refrigerator for up to 1 week or in the freezer for up to a year.

Chef's Tip: *Kombu and bonito flakes can be found at Asian markets or online.*

WILD MUSHROOM BROTH

YIELD: 2 quarts | **PREP TIME:** 10 minutes
STOVETOP: 45 minutes | **SLOW COOKER:** 6 to 8 hours | **PRESSURE COOKER:** 25 minutes

1 ounce dried wild mushrooms (about 1 full cup)

1 ounce dried shiitake mushrooms (about 1 full cup)

1 pound assorted fresh mushrooms and/or mushroom stems and trimmings

1 leek, cleaned and chopped (see Tip on page 38)

1 carrot, chopped

1 celery rib, chopped

1 sheet nori

10 to 12 black peppercorns

5 sprigs fresh thyme

1 bay leaf

1 teaspoon salt

AIP Modification: *Omit the peppercorns.*

01 Place all of the ingredients in a large pot and cover with 10 cups of cool water. Bring to a simmer and cook, uncovered, for about 45 minutes, until the broth has reduced by about 2 cups.

02 Use a fine-mesh strainer to strain the broth. Strain a second time through cheesecloth if any sediment remains. Store the broth in a glass jar in the refrigerator for up to 1 week or in the freezer for up to a year.

 Slow Cooker Instructions: *Place all of the ingredients in a slow cooker and cover with 2 quarts of cool water. Cook on low for 6 to 8 hours. Proceed with Step 2.*

 Pressure Cooker Instructions: *Place all of the ingredients in a pressure cooker and cover with 2 quarts of cool water. Secure the lid and cook on low pressure for 15 minutes, then allow the pressure to release naturally for 10 minutes before opening the lid. Proceed with Step 2.*

FISH BROTH

YIELD: 2 quarts | PREP TIME: 10 minutes
STOVETOP: about 1 hour | SLOW COOKER: 6 to 8 hours | PRESSURE COOKER: 20 minutes

2 pounds fish bones and heads (preferably from lean white fish such as halibut, cod, or flounder)

1 tablespoon apple cider vinegar

1 large onion, peeled and quartered

2 cloves garlic, unpeeled, whacked with the side of a knife

2 small parsnips, peeled and chopped

1 celery rib, chopped

3 to 4 parsley stems

1 teaspoon salt

10 to 12 black peppercorns

AIP Modification: *Omit the peppercorns.*

01 Place all of the ingredients in a large pot and cover with 3 quarts of cool water. Bring to a boil. Cook until the foam starts to rise to the top; when it does, skim it off with a spoon or ladle.

02 After you've skimmed the foam, turn the heat down to medium-low so that the broth is at a simmer. Cook for 45 minutes, uncovered, until the liquid has reduced by about one-third.

03 Use a fine-mesh strainer to strain the broth, pressing as much liquid from the bones and vegetables as possible before discarding them. Store the broth in a glass jar in the refrigerator for up to 4 days or in the freezer for up to 6 months.

 Slow Cooker Instructions: *Place all of the ingredients in a slow cooker and cover with 2 quarts of cool water. Cook on low for 6 to 8 hours. Continue with Step 3.*

 Pressure Cooker Instructions: *Place all of the ingredients in a pressure cooker and cover with 2 quarts of cool water. Secure the lid and cook on high pressure for 20 minutes. Quick-release the pressure and continue with Step 3.*

SHRIMP CILANTRO BROTH

YIELD: 2 quarts | **PREP TIME:** 5 minutes
STOVETOP: 1 hour | **SLOW COOKER:** 6 to 8 hours | **PRESSURE COOKER:** 20 minutes

Shells from 1 pound shrimp

Tops from 1 bunch green onions

Stems from 1 bunch cilantro

2 tablespoons unseasoned rice vinegar

1 teaspoon salt

10 to 12 black peppercorns

AIP Modification: *Omit the peppercorns.*

01 Place all of the ingredients in a large pot. Add 3 quarts of cool water and bring to a simmer. Simmer, uncovered, for 1 hour.

02 Strain the broth through a fine-mesh strainer and pour into jars until ready to use. Store the broth in a glass jar in the refrigerator for up to 1 week or in the freezer for up to a year.

 Slow Cooker Instructions: *Place all of the ingredients in a slow cooker and cover with 2 quarts of cool water. Cook on low for 6 to 8 hours. Continue with Step 2.*

 Pressure Cooker Instructions: *Place all of the ingredients in a pressure cooker and cover with 2 quarts of cool water. Secure the lid and cook on high pressure for 20 minutes. Quick-release the pressure and continue with Step 2.*

PHO BROTH

YIELD: 2 quarts | **PREP TIME:** 5 minutes
STOVETOP: about 6 hours | **SLOW COOKER:** about 11 to 13 hours | **PRESSURE COOKER:** 2 hours 15 minutes

This broth recipe was developed with Classic Beef Pho (page 104) in mind, so it uses beef parts that are best suited for that recipe. However, the broth itself is so incredibly flavorful, you might find that it's your favorite for sipping. It's also wonderful served with Wontons (page 192) or Wrapper-Less Wontons (page 200), or as the base for an extra-flavorful Egg Drop Soup (page 130). If you don't plan on making pho or otherwise using the meat that is left over after making this broth, it can be frozen for up to 6 months.

2 large onions, cut lengthwise into 3 or 4 slices

1 (4-inch) piece fresh ginger, sliced in half lengthwise

3 pounds beef shank, with meat

2½ pounds oxtail

1½ pounds boneless chuck

2 tablespoons apple cider vinegar

1 cinnamon stick

3 star anise

6 whole cloves

1 teaspoon coriander seeds

1 teaspoon black peppercorns

1 tablespoon coconut sugar

1 teaspoon salt

01 Position an oven rack in the top position and preheat the broiler. Place the onions and ginger on a rimmed baking sheet and broil for 5 minutes. Rotate the pan 180 degrees and broil for another 5 minutes. Flip the onions and ginger and broil for another 5 minutes. Rotate the pan 180 degrees and roast for another 5 minutes. The onion and ginger should be deeply charred, which will take about 20 to 25 minutes total.

02 While the onion and ginger are under the broiler, put the beef shank, oxtail, and chuck in a large pot and cover with cool water. Bring to a boil. Boil for 15 minutes, then strain the beef parts and discard the water. Rinse the beef parts under cold running water.

03 Rinse out the pot, then return the beef parts to it. Cover the beef parts with about 3 quarts of fresh cold water, or more if necessary to cover the bones. Add the charred onions and ginger and the remaining ingredients. Bring to a simmer and let simmer for 1 to 1½ hours, until the chuck is tender but not falling apart.

04 Remove the beef chuck from the pot and refrigerate until ready to serve. Continue to cook the broth for another 4 hours, adding more water if necessary to keep the beef parts completely covered.

05 Strain the broth through a fine-mesh strainer. Reserve the meat from the oxtail and shank for use in Classic Beef Pho (page 104), if desired. Store the broth in a glass jar in the refrigerator for up to 1 week or in the freezer for up to a year.

Slow Cooker Instructions: *After completing Step 2, transfer the beef parts, onions, and ginger to a slow cooker and add the remaining ingredients and 2 quarts of cool water. Cook on low for 10 to 12 hours. Continue with Step 5.*

 Pressure Cooker Instructions: *After completing Step 2, transfer the beef parts, onions, and ginger to a pressure cooker and add the remaining ingredients and 2 quarts of cool water. Pour in just enough water to cover the bones and meat. Secure the lid and cook on high pressure for 30 minutes. Quick-release the pressure. Remove the chuck and refrigerate. Secure the lid again and cook on high for an additional 75 minutes. Allow the pressure to release naturally for 10 minutes before opening the lid, then continue with Step 5.*

CASHEW CREAM

YIELD: 3 cups | PREP TIME: less than 5 minutes, plus 4 hours to soak the cashews

The thickness and neutral flavor of cashew cream make it a great stand-in for heavy cream for those who don't tolerate dairy.

1 cup raw cashews

01 Soak the cashews in 2 to 3 cups of cool water for at least 4 hours or up to overnight. Refrigerate if soaking for more than 4 hours.

02 Drain the cashews and place them in a blender along with 2 cups of cool fresh water. Blend until very smooth.

03 Store the cream in a glass jar in the fridge for up to 5 days.

FLAX MILK

 YIELD: 2 cups | **PREP TIME:** less than 5 minutes

If you don't tolerate dairy or nuts, making creamy soups can be tricky. Coconut milk is great, but it just doesn't work with every flavor profile. Flax milk is a nice nut-free alternative in any of the soups in this book that call for cashew cream. It's widely available in grocery stores with the other dairy-free milks, and it's easy to make at home as well.

2 tablespoons flax seeds
Pinch of salt

01 In a blender, combine the flax seeds, salt, and 2 cups of water. Blend on high speed for about 30 seconds.

02 Strain the flax milk through a nut milk bag or a fine-mesh strainer lined with two layers of cheesecloth.

03 Store in the fridge and use within 4 days.

DAIRY-FREE YOGURT AND SOUR CREAM

YIELD: 1½ cups | PREP TIME: 5 minutes, plus time to soak the cashews | CULTURING TIME: 8 hours

Yogurt is a great condiment and addition to a lot of soups, and now you can make a dairy-free version easily at home. Culturing cashew puree gives it an authentic yogurt flavor, along with the benefits that come with it! If you do tolerate dairy and would rather use that, I recommend purchasing full-fat yogurt or sour cream without any sweeteners or additives.

2 cups raw cashews, soaked in 1 quart water for at least 4 hours or overnight

25 billion organisms probiotics

FOR YOGURT:

1 teaspoon maple syrup (optional)

FOR SOUR CREAM:

1 to 2 teaspoons fresh lemon juice or mild-tasting vinegar

01 Drain the cashews and place them in a food processor or blender (a twister jar works best for this recipe). Add 1 cup of water and blend until completely smooth, scraping down the sides several times.

02 Transfer the mixture to a small saucepan and heat it to 120°F. Stir constantly while heating so it doesn't burn. Stir in the probiotics.

03 Pour the mixture into a 12-ounce canning jar. Leave the jar uncovered.

04 If using a multi-cooker: Pour ½ cup of water into the insert and put the steamer rack in the multi-cooker. Place the jar on the rack and press the yogurt setting. Adjust the time to 8 hours if it doesn't automatically set to that.

If using your oven: Set the jar in the oven and turn on the light. Leave for at least 8 hours.

05 After 8 hours, remove the jar from the multi-cooker or oven. If making yogurt, stir in the maple syrup, if using. If making sour cream, stir in the lemon juice. Place the lid on the jar and refrigerate. Use within 5 days.

CHAPTER 2

BLENDED SOUPS

The lovely thing about blended soups is that you get all of the flavors in each and every spoonful. These are often the quickest soups to make—and they can sometimes be made with water instead of broth. Of course, broth adds a nutritional component, so I do recommend using it whenever possible, but if that thing called real life is happening and you have about 30 minutes to get some tomato soup on the table, don't sweat it.

There are two ways to blend soup: in a jar blender or with an immersion blender. An immersion blender creates fewer dirty dishes, since the pureeing can be done right in the cooking pot. This results in a somewhat coarser-textured soup but is great for Super Green Soup (page 68), Mushroom Bisque (page 86), and both of the tomato soups (pages 74 and 76). If an immersion blender is your tool of choice, you can definitely use it for every recipe in this chapter, but you might need to spend a little extra time blending to get a smooth texture.

Using a high-powered jar blender will yield a velvety puree that is nothing short of luxurious. When blending hot liquids in a jar blender, please be careful, and follow these instructions:

- Don't fill the blender more than halfway; puree the soup in batches if needed.

- Place a folded towel over the top of the lid and vent a corner of the lid a tiny bit to allow steam to escape.

- Start at a slow speed and increase it gradually.

- Use a towel to open the lid after blending in case there is any spray.

FRENCH SQUASH SOUP
with pears and herbes de Provence

YIELD: 4 to 6 servings | PREP TIME: 5 minutes
STOVETOP: about 1 hour 30 minutes | SLOW COOKER: 6 to 8 hours | PRESSURE COOKER: 25 minutes

2 medium butternut, acorn, or kabocha squash, or a combination

2 tablespoons melted ghee or avocado oil, divided

2 teaspoons salt, divided

1 teaspoon ground black pepper

1 large onion, chopped

2 pears, peeled, cored, and diced

6 cups Chicken Broth (page 40)

1 teaspoon herbes de Provence

Fresh tarragon, for garnish (optional)

AIP Modification: *Use avocado oil or olive oil instead of ghee and omit the black pepper.*

01 Preheat the oven to 425°F. Cut the squash in half and scoop out the seeds. Brush the cut sides with 1 tablespoon of the ghee and sprinkle with 1 teaspoon of the salt and the pepper. Place the squash cut side up on a baking sheet and roast for 60 to 75 minutes, until very soft. Set aside to cool.

02 About 15 minutes before the squash is done roasting, heat the remaining tablespoon of ghee in a large pot over medium heat. When the ghee is hot, add the onion and the remaining teaspoon of salt and sauté, stirring occasionally, for 8 to 10 minutes, until golden brown and softened. Add the pears and cook for another 5 minutes.

03 When the squash is cool enough to handle, scoop out the flesh and add it to the pot with the onions and pears. Add the broth and herbes de Provence and bring to a boil. Reduce the heat to a simmer and cook for 10 minutes, or until the pears are very soft.

04 Puree the soup in batches in a blender until smooth. Garnish with tarragon, if desired.

 Slow Cooker Instructions: *Instead of roasting the squash, peel and cut it into large dice. After completing Step 2, transfer the onion and pears to a slow cooker. Add the diced squash, salt, pepper, chicken broth, and herbes de Provence and cook on low for 6 to 8 hours. Proceed with Step 4.*

 Pressure Cooker Instructions: *Instead of roasting the squash, peel and cut it into large dice. After completing Step 2, transfer the onion and pears to a pressure cooker. Add the diced squash, salt, pepper, chicken broth, and herbes de Provence and cook on high pressure for 15 minutes. Quick-release the pressure and proceed with Step 4.*

GREAT WITH

Baguette slices

SUPER GREEN SOUP

 YIELD: 4 to 6 servings | PREP TIME: 10 minutes | STOVETOP: 25 minutes

2 small leeks

1 large head broccoli

1 tablespoon ghee, light olive oil, or avocado oil

1 teaspoon salt

3 cloves garlic, chopped

1 quart Chicken Broth (page 40) or Roasted Vegetable Broth (page 36)

1 bunch spinach or 8 ounces baby spinach

Chopped fresh chives, for garnish (optional)

AIP Modification: *Use avocado oil instead of ghee or olive oil.*

01 Cut the root ends off the leeks, then cut them in half lengthwise and rinse out any dirt. Slice the white and light green parts into half-moons. Cut the broccoli stalk into coins and the crown into florets.

02 Heat the ghee in a large pot over medium heat. When hot, add the leeks, broccoli coins, and salt. Cook until the veggies are softened, about 10 minutes. You want the veggies to sweat but not brown. If they start to brown, add a small amount of the broth and continue cooking.

03 Add the broccoli florets and garlic and cook for another 4 to 5 minutes, until the garlic is fragrant.

04 Add the broth and cover the pot. Bring to a simmer, then cook until the broccoli is very soft, about 10 minutes. Add the spinach and cook until just wilted.

05 Puree the soup in batches in a blender or with an immersion blender until smooth.

06 Serve garnished with chopped chives, if desired.

MOROCCAN CARROT SOUP
with yogurt and mace

 YIELD: 4 to 6 servings | **PREP TIME:** 10 minutes | **STOVETOP:** about 40 minutes

1 tablespoon avocado oil or light olive oil

1 medium onion, diced

1 tablespoon grated fresh ginger

2 teaspoons grated fresh turmeric or ¾ teaspoon turmeric powder

½ teaspoon ground coriander

½ teaspoon ground cumin

⅛ teaspoon ground cinnamon

1 teaspoon salt

2 pounds carrots, chopped

1 apple, peeled, cored, and diced

6 cups Chicken Broth (page 40) or Roasted Vegetable Broth (page 36)

Dairy-Free Yogurt (page 62) or Spiced Yogurt (page 220), for garnish

Ground mace, for garnish

01 In a large pot, heat the oil over medium-high heat. When the oil is hot, add the onion and cook for 6 to 8 minutes, until golden brown and beginning to soften.

02 Turn the heat down to low. Add the ginger, turmeric, coriander, cumin, cinnamon, and salt and cook for another minute, or until fragrant, stirring constantly.

03 Add the carrots, apple, and broth and bring to a boil. Turn the heat down to medium-low and cover. Simmer for 30 minutes, or until the carrots are very soft.

04 Puree the soup in batches in a blender until smooth. Garnish each serving with a swirl of yogurt and a sprinkling of ground mace.

AIP Modification: *Omit the coriander, cumin, and yogurt. Garnish with coconut cream instead, if desired.*

ASPARAGUS BISQUE
with cayenne and lime

 YIELD: 4 to 6 servings | PREP TIME: 10 minutes | STOVETOP: 15 minutes

3 tablespoons ghee or avocado oil

4 small leeks, white and light green parts only, cleaned and sliced crosswise (see Tip on page 38)

2 teaspoons salt

4 bunches asparagus (about 4 pounds), woody ends removed, chopped

3 cloves garlic, chopped

1 quart Veggie-Herb Broth (page 38) or Chicken Broth (page 40)

¼ teaspoon cayenne pepper

¼ cup fresh lime juice (about 2 limes)

Strips of lime zest, for garnish (optional)

01 Heat the ghee in a large pot over medium heat. When the ghee is melted, add the leeks and salt and sweat for 5 minutes, or until the leeks begin to soften. Add the asparagus and garlic and cook for another 5 minutes.

02 Add the broth and cayenne pepper and cook until the asparagus is soft, 3 to 4 minutes. Stir in the lime juice. Puree the soup in batches in a blender or with an immersion blender until smooth. Season to taste with additional cayenne pepper and/or lime juice, if desired, and garnish with strips of lime zest, if using.

AIP Modification: *Omit the cayenne pepper.*

CREAMY TOMATO BASIL SOUP

 YIELD: 4 to 6 servings | PREP TIME: 5 minutes | STOVETOP: 20 minutes

1 tablespoon ghee or avocado oil

1 large onion, sliced

6 cloves garlic, peeled

1 teaspoon salt

½ teaspoon garlic powder

2 (28-ounce) cans diced tomatoes or 4 pounds fresh tomatoes (see page 21 for prep instructions)

2 cups Chicken Broth (page 40) or water

½ cup roughly chopped fresh basil leaves, plus more for garnish (garnish optional)

1 cup full-fat coconut milk

Ground black pepper

01   In a large heavy-bottomed pot, heat the ghee over medium heat. When the ghee is hot, add the onion slices, garlic, salt, and garlic powder. Cook, stirring often, until the onions are softened, about 8 minutes.

02   Add the tomatoes and broth and bring to a boil. Once boiling, reduce the heat to medium-low, cover, and simmer for 10 minutes.

03   Add the basil and coconut milk, then puree the soup in batches in a blender or with an immersion blender. Season to taste with salt and pepper. Garnish each bowl with a few basil leaves, if desired.

GREAT WITH

Croutons

Breadsticks

246
Baguette slices

TOMATO AND ROASTED PEPPER SOUP

 YIELD: 4 to 6 servings | PREP TIME: 5 minutes | STOVETOP: 20 minutes

1 tablespoon ghee or avocado oil

1 large onion, sliced

6 cloves garlic, peeled

1 teaspoon salt

½ teaspoon garlic powder

2 (28-ounce) cans diced tomatoes or 4 pounds fresh tomatoes (see page 21 for prep instructions)

2 whole roasted red peppers, roughly chopped

2 cups Chicken Broth (page 40) or water

¼ cup roughly chopped fresh cilantro

Ground black pepper

Lime wedges, for serving (optional)

01 In a large heavy-bottomed pot, heat the ghee over medium heat. When the ghee is hot, add the onion, garlic, salt, and garlic powder and stir to combine. Cook, stirring often, until the onion is softened, about 8 minutes.

02 Add the tomatoes, roasted peppers, and broth and bring to a boil. Turn the heat down to medium-low, cover, and simmer for 10 minutes.

03 Add the cilantro, then puree the soup in batches in a blender or with an immersion blender. Season to taste with pepper and more salt, if needed. Serve with lime wedges, if desired.

GREAT WITH

Flour Tortillas or Crispy Tortilla Chips *Plantain Tortillas*

ROASTED CAULIFLOWER SOUP
with lime and pine nuts

 YIELD: 4 to 6 servings | **PREP TIME:** 15 minutes | **STOVETOP:** about 45 minutes

1 head cauliflower (about 2 pounds), cut into thick slices (no need to core it)

1 large onion, cut into thick slices

2 tablespoons melted ghee or avocado oil

3 tablespoons pine nuts

1 quart Chicken Broth (page 40), plus more if needed

1 teaspoon salt

1/4 teaspoon ground black pepper

2 tablespoons fresh lime juice

Grated zest of 1 lime

AIP Modification: *Use avocado oil instead of ghee and omit the pine nuts and black pepper.*

Nut-Free Modification: *Omit the pine nuts.*

01 Preheat the oven to 450°F.

02 On a rimmed baking sheet, toss the cauliflower and onion with the melted ghee. Roast for 30 to 35 minutes, until caramelized, turning the vegetables halfway through cooking.

03 While the veggies are roasting, toast the pine nuts in a small dry skillet over medium-low heat for 3 to 5 minutes, stirring often. They will start to release their oils and then start to brown. When they start to brown, remove them from the pan and set aside.

04 Transfer the roasted vegetables to a large pot and add just enough broth to cover the vegetables. Pour a small amount of broth onto the roasting pan and scrape with a spatula to release any stuck-on bits. Add that liquid to the pot as well. Bring to a simmer and cook for 10 to 15 minutes, until the cauliflower is very soft.

05 Puree the soup in batches in a blender or use an immersion blender. Add more broth as needed to obtain the desired consistency.

06 Add the salt and pepper, then taste for seasoning, adding more if desired.

07 Before serving, add the lime juice and garnish with the lime zest and toasted pine nuts.

BURNT BROCCOLI SOUP
with lemon

 YIELD: 4 to 6 servings | **PREP TIME:** 10 minutes | **STOVETOP:** 30 minutes

2 pounds broccoli

4 tablespoons melted duck fat or avocado oil, divided

2 leeks, cleaned and sliced crosswise (see Tip on page 38)

1 teaspoon salt

4 cloves garlic, chopped

Zest of 1 lemon, grated or cut into fine strips

4 to 5 cups Chicken Broth (page 40) or Veggie-Herb Broth (page 38)

1 tablespoon fresh lemon juice

1 tablespoon extra-virgin olive oil, plus more for garnish

01 Preheat the broiler to high and position an oven rack about 6 inches below the flame.

02 Cut the broccoli heads into large florets. Slice the stems into 1/2-inch-thick rounds and set aside for use in Step 4.

03 Toss the florets with 3 tablespoons of the duck fat and place under the broiler. Broil for about 10 minutes, without stirring, until the broccoli is browned.

04 While the broccoli is broiling, heat the remaining tablespoon of duck fat in a large pot over medium heat. When the fat is hot, add the leeks, broccoli stems, and salt. Sweat the veggies for 5 minutes, stirring occasionally. Add the garlic and cook for 1 minute.

05 Add most of the lemon zest (reserve some for garnish), the broccoli florets, and 4 cups of the broth to the pot. Bring to a simmer, cover, and simmer over medium heat for 15 minutes, or until the broccoli is very soft.

06 Add the lemon juice and olive oil. Puree the soup in batches in a blender or with an immersion blender, adding up to 1 cup more broth if necessary to achieve the desired consistency. Garnish with the reserved lemon zest and a drizzle of olive oil.

GREAT WITH

 208 212 226

Rosemary-Garlic Oil   Croutons   Seeded Crackers

30 CLOVES OF GARLIC SOUP

 YIELD: 4 to 6 servings | **PREP TIME:** 15 minutes | **STOVETOP:** about 35 minutes

2 heads cauliflower (about 3 pounds total), cut into florets

Cloves from 2 heads garlic, unpeeled

3 tablespoons melted ghee or avocado oil

6 cups Chicken Broth (page 40)

1 teaspoon salt

Sliced fresh chives, for garnish (optional)

AIP Modification: *Use avocado oil instead of ghee.*

01 Preheat the oven to 425°F.

02 Toss the cauliflower and garlic with the ghee and place on a rimmed baking sheet. Roast for 30 to 35 minutes, stirring once, until the cauliflower is browned and the garlic is soft.

03 When the veggies are cool enough to handle, squeeze the garlic out of their papery peels into a blender. Add the cauliflower, broth, and salt and puree until smooth, in batches if necessary.

04 Transfer the soup to a large pot and place over medium heat until warmed through, about 5 minutes. Serve garnished with chives, if desired.

GREAT WITH

| Pesto | Rosemary-Garlic Oil | Croutons | Toasted Baguette slices |

POTATO LEEK SOUP
with frizzled leeks

YIELD: 4 to 6 servings | PREP TIME: 10 minutes
STOVETOP: 40 minutes | SLOW COOKER: 6 to 8 hours | PRESSURE COOKER: 20 minutes

2 tablespoons ghee or light olive oil

1½ pounds leeks (about 3 medium), white and light green parts only, cleaned and cut into ½-inch pieces (see Tip on page 38)

1 teaspoon salt

2 pounds russet potatoes (about 4 large), peeled and chopped

1 quart Roasted Vegetable Broth (page 36) or Chicken Broth (page 40)

1 bay leaf

1¼ cups Cashew Cream (page 58)

1 tablespoon fresh lemon juice

1 batch Frizzled Leeks (page 216), for garnish

Nut-Free Modification: *Use coconut milk or flax milk (page 60) instead of cashew cream.*

01 In a large heavy-bottomed pot over medium heat, melt the ghee. Add the leeks and salt and cook, stirring occasionally, for 10 minutes, or until very soft.

02 Add the potatoes, broth, and bay leaf and bring to a boil. Cook until the potatoes are very soft, about 30 minutes.

03 Remove the bay leaf and puree the soup in batches in a blender or with an immersion blender. Stir in the cashew cream and lemon juice and cook for an additional minute or two, just to heat through.

04 Serve garnished with Frizzled Leeks.

Slow Cooker Instructions: *After completing Step 1, put the sautéed leeks in a slow cooker along with the potatoes, broth, and bay leaf. Cook on low for 6 to 8 hours, until the potatoes are very soft. Continue with Step 3.*

Pressure Cooker Instructions: *After completing Step 1, put the sautéed leeks in a pressure cooker along with the potatoes, broth, and bay leaf. Secure the lid and cook on high pressure for 10 minutes. Allow the pressure to release naturally for 10 minutes before opening the lid. Continue with Step 3.*

MUSHROOM BISQUE

 YIELD: 4 to 6 servings | PREP TIME: 20 minutes | STOVETOP: 20 minutes

2 tablespoons ghee or unsalted butter

2 tablespoons extra-virgin olive oil

1 cup chopped shallots (about 2 large)

2 tablespoons arrowroot starch

1 pound button mushrooms, roughly chopped

½ pound cremini mushrooms, roughly chopped

½ pound shiitake mushrooms, roughly chopped

3 cloves garlic, sliced

1 teaspoon fresh thyme leaves, plus more for garnish

1 teaspoon salt

½ cup plus 1 tablespoon dry sherry, divided

6 cups Wild Mushroom Broth (page 50)

¾ cup heavy cream or Cashew Cream (page 58)

¼ to ½ teaspoon truffle salt (optional)

01 In a large pot, heat the ghee and olive oil over medium-high heat. When the ghee is hot, add the shallots and cook for 3 to 4 minutes, until softened and just starting to brown. Stir in the arrowroot starch and cook for another minute, stirring constantly.

02 Add the chopped mushrooms, garlic, thyme, and salt. Cook for about 5 minutes, until the mushrooms release their liquid. If the mixture starts to burn on the bottom of the pot, move on to Step 3.

03 Add ½ cup of the sherry, scraping up any browned bits on the bottom of the pot. Cook for 1 to 2 minutes, until the liquid is mostly gone.

04 Add the broth and bring to a simmer. Cook for 10 minutes. Puree the soup in batches in a blender and return it to the pot, or puree it right in the pot with an immersion blender. Stir in the cream and the remaining tablespoon of sherry.

05 Season to taste with salt, or use truffle salt if desired. Serve garnished with thyme leaves and truffle salt, if desired.

AIP Modification: *Use avocado oil instead of ghee or butter and use coconut milk instead of heavy cream or cashew cream.*

Nut-Free Modification: *Use coconut milk or flax milk (page 60) instead of heavy cream or cashew cream.*

GREAT WITH

212

228

246

Croutons   *Garlic and Chive Crackers*   *Toasted Baguette slices*

THAI PUMPKIN SOUP

YIELD: 4 to 6 servings | PREP TIME: 20 minutes
STOVETOP: 1 hour | SLOW COOKER: 3 to 4 or 8 to 10 hours | PRESSURE COOKER: about 45 minutes

1 sugar pumpkin (about 3½ pounds) or 4 cups canned pumpkin puree

2 tablespoons coconut oil, divided

3 (6-inch) sections lemongrass, chopped (about ¼ cup)

1 thumb-size piece fresh ginger, peeled and grated

1 serrano chile or jalapeño pepper, seeded and chopped

1 cup chopped shallots (about 2 large)

1 teaspoon salt

6 fresh kaffir lime leaves, veins removed (see Tip)

1 (14-ounce) can full-fat coconut milk

3 cups Chicken Broth (page 40)

Sliced fresh Thai basil leaves, for garnish (optional)

Chef's Tip: *If you can't find kaffir lime leaves, use the zest of 1 lime instead.*

AIP Modification: *Omit the serrano chile.*

01 If using canned pumpkin puree, skip ahead to Step 2. Preheat the oven to 375°F. With a sharp knife, cut the stem off the pumpkin and slice the pumpkin in half lengthwise. Scoop out the seeds. Rub the inside of the pumpkin with 1 tablespoon of the coconut oil and place it cut side down on a rimmed baking sheet. Roast for 30 to 40 minutes, until very soft. When the pumpkin is cool enough to handle, remove the flesh from the skin and discard the skin. While you're waiting for the pumpkin to cool, prepare the rest of the ingredients.

02 Heat the remaining tablespoon of coconut oil in a large heavy-bottomed pot over medium heat. When the oil is hot, add the lemongrass, ginger, serrano chile, and shallots. Stir in the salt and sauté for 5 to 7 minutes, until the mixture is fragrant and the shallots are translucent. If they start to brown, turn down the heat.

03 Add the kaffir lime leaves and coconut milk and turn the heat up to high. Boil for 5 minutes, then add the pumpkin and broth. Return the soup to a boil, then turn the heat down to medium-low and simmer, covered, for 20 minutes.

04 Puree the soup in batches in a blender or with an immersion blender. Add additional salt, if needed. Garnish with Thai basil, if desired.

 Slow Cooker Instructions: *After completing Step 2, transfer the contents of the pot, along with the pumpkin and remaining ingredients, to a slow cooker. Cover and cook on high for 3 to 4 hours or on low for 8 to 10 hours. Proceed with Step 4.*

 Pressure Cooker Instructions: *After completing Step 2, transfer the contents of the pot, along with the pumpkin and remaining ingredients, to a pressure cooker. Secure the lid and set it to high pressure for 8 minutes. Vent to quick-release the pressure and then open the lid. Proceed with Step 4.*

GREAT WITH

Dairy-Free Yogurt 62

Curry Coconut Cream 210

Spiced Pepitas 214

SWEET POTATO SOUP
with chipotle and lime

 YIELD: 4 to 6 servings | PREP TIME: 10 minutes | STOVETOP: 20 minutes

1 tablespoon avocado oil or coconut oil

1 large onion, diced

5 pounds sweet potatoes (about 6 large), peeled and chopped

2 teaspoons salt

1 teaspoon ground coriander

1 teaspoon ground cumin

1 teaspoon smoked paprika

¼ to ½ teaspoon chipotle chili powder

¼ cup fresh lime juice (about 2 limes)

Chopped fresh cilantro, for garnish

01 In a large heavy-bottomed pot, heat the oil over medium-high heat. When the oil is hot, add the onion and sauté, stirring occasionally, for 6 to 8 minutes, until golden brown and softened. Add the sweet potatoes, salt, coriander, cumin, smoked paprika, and chipotle powder.

02 Add 6 cups of cool water and bring to a simmer. Simmer for 10 to 12 minutes, until the sweet potatoes are very soft. Puree until smooth, either in batches in a blender or with an immersion blender. Stir in the lime juice and garnish with cilantro.

GREAT WITH

Spiced Pepitas   Spiced Yogurt   Flour Tortillas   Plantain Tortillas

CHAPTER 3

HEARTY SOUPS

"I could eat chicken soup every day."
—My grandma Helen

She said that every time she ate a bowl of chicken soup. The funny thing is, now I find myself saying the exact same thing. Not only could I eat it every day, but I could eat it for breakfast, lunch, or dinner. While chicken soup may always be my favorite, just about any bowl of hearty soup tends to give me the warm fuzzies.

The soups in this chapter represent flavors from all over the world, with inspiration from the cuisines of China, Burma, Thailand, Vietnam, Italy, Eastern Europe, France, Spain, and Portugal, and of course there are plenty of American classics and California fusion recipes as well. After all, what brings the flavors of a region (or multiple regions) together the way soup does?

The recipes in this chapter range from great weeknight supper soups, like Tom Yum (page 100) and Italian Wedding Soup (page 110), to soups that are better suited for a Sunday project, like Lobster Bisque (page 142) and Oxtail and Smoked Pork Gumbo (page 144). And of course, there are a lot of soups that fall somewhere in between, taking about an hour to get onto the table. If you're short on time, look for the ⏱ icon, which marks those soups that take one hour or less to make from start to finish.

SPRING CHICKEN SOUP
with lemon and asparagus

 YIELD: 4 to 6 servings | **PREP TIME:** 15 minutes | **STOVETOP:** about 50 minutes

1 whole bone-in, skin-on chicken breast (about 2 pounds)

½ teaspoon herbes de Provence

½ teaspoon salt

1 tablespoon avocado oil

1 medium onion, thinly sliced

¾ pound asparagus, ends trimmed, cut into ½-inch pieces

2 cloves garlic, sliced

6 cups Chicken Broth (page 40)

1 cup chopped watercress (about 1 bunch)

1 pound zucchini or yellow squash (or a combination), made into wide ribbons with a vegetable peeler or spiral slicer

¼ cup chopped fresh basil, plus more for garnish

1 tablespoon fresh lemon juice

Lemon wedges, for serving

01 Preheat the oven to 425°F.

02 Lift the skin of the chicken and rub the meat underneath with the herbes de Provence and salt. Place the chicken on a rimmed baking sheet and roast for 40 minutes, or until cooked through with an internal temperature of 160°F. Once cool enough to handle, remove the meat from the bones and chop it.

03 Heat the oil in a large heavy-bottomed pot over medium-high heat. When the oil is hot, add the onion and cook for 5 minutes, or until translucent, stirring often.

04 Add the asparagus and garlic and cook for 2 minutes, or until the garlic is fragrant.

05 Add the broth and bring to a simmer. Cook until the asparagus is tender, 1 to 2 minutes.

06 Add the chicken, watercress, zucchini ribbons, and basil and cook for 1 minute, or until just heated through. Stir in the lemon juice and add salt to taste.

07 Serve garnished with extra chopped basil, and with lemon wedges on the side.

HARVEST CHICKEN SOUP
with sweet potato gnocchi

YIELD: 4 to 6 servings | PREP TIME: 20 minutes | STOVETOP: 55 minutes | SLOW COOKER: 8 to 10 hours

1 large onion, diced

3 celery ribs, diced

3 large carrots, diced

2 medium parsnips, peeled and diced

6 cloves garlic, unpeeled

2 tablespoons extra-virgin olive oil, divided

1 teaspoon salt, divided

Ground black pepper

1 whole bone-in, skin-on chicken breast (about 2 pounds)

2 quarts Chicken Broth (page 40)

1/2 pound kale, stemmed and torn or chopped into 1-inch pieces

1/2 teaspoon minced fresh thyme (about 4 sprigs)

1 batch cooked Sweet Potato Gnocchi (page 202) or 4 to 6 servings cooked spaghetti squash noodles or sweet potato noodles (page 194)

2 tablespoons pomegranate arils

AIP Modification: *Omit the black pepper and serve with veggie noodles instead of gnocchi.*

Lower-Carb / Egg-Free / Nut-Free Modification: *Serve with veggie noodles instead of gnocchi.*

01 Preheat the oven to 425°F.

02 In a large baking dish, toss the diced veggies and garlic with 1 tablespoon of the olive oil and 1/2 teaspoon of the salt.

03 Season the chicken with the remaining 1/2 teaspoon of salt and a few grinds of black pepper. Rub the remaining tablespoon of olive oil all over the chicken. Place the chicken on top of the veggies and roast for 40 to 45 minutes, until the chicken reaches an internal temperature of 160°F and the veggies are brown and softened.

04 Remove the chicken and place in the fridge to cool. Squeeze the garlic cloves out of their peels and mash lightly.

05 Add the roasted veggies and garlic to a large pot along with the broth, kale, and thyme. Bring to a simmer and cook for 10 minutes, or until the kale is soft.

06 While the soup simmers, pull the chicken meat off the bone and cut or tear it into bite-sized pieces. Discard the skin and bones or reserve the bones for making broth. Add the chicken to the soup, along with the gnocchi or your preferred noodle, and simmer for 1 to 2 minutes, until just heated through. Serve garnished with pomegranate arils.

Slow Cooker Instructions: *Peel the garlic cloves and toss them and the vegetables with 1/2 teaspoon of salt, a few pinches of pepper, and 1 tablespoon of olive oil. Place in a slow cooker, along with the kale and thyme. Season the chicken with 1/2 teaspoon of salt, a couple pinches of pepper, and 1 tablespoon of olive oil and place on top of the vegetables. Pour in the broth and cook on low for 8 to 10 hours. Remove the chicken and, once cool enough to handle, pull the meat off the bone. Cut or tear the chicken into bite-sized pieces and return to the pot. Add the gnocchi or noodles to heat through. Serve garnished with pomegranate arils.*

Chef's Tip: *Use leftover roast chicken and a variety of leftover roasted veggies to make a super-quick soup. Just simmer the veggies in the broth for 10 minutes as directed in Step 5, then add 3 cups of cooked chicken and heat through.*

SWEET AND SOUR CABBAGE SOUP

 YIELD: 4 to 6 servings | PREP TIME: 10 minutes | STOVETOP: 20 minutes | SLOW COOKER: 8 to 10 hours

1 tablespoon light olive oil or avocado oil

1 medium head cabbage (about 2 pounds), chopped

1 large onion, diced

1 teaspoon salt

2 tablespoons tomato paste

1 (14-ounce) can diced tomatoes or 1 pound fresh tomatoes (see page 21 for prep instructions)

¼ cup apple cider vinegar

2 tablespoons honey

1 teaspoon paprika

½ teaspoon cayenne pepper

2 quarts Basic Beef Broth (page 42)

01 Heat the oil in a large pot over medium-high heat. When the oil is hot, add the cabbage, onion, and salt. Cook for about 10 minutes, until the cabbage is wilted.

02 Stir in the tomato paste and cook for another minute, then add the tomatoes, vinegar, honey, paprika, cayenne pepper, and broth. Bring to a simmer and cook for 10 minutes, or until the onion and cabbage are very tender.

03 Taste for seasoning. The soup should have a nice balance of sweet and sour with a little bit of a kick. Add more honey, vinegar, or cayenne pepper as desired.

 Slow Cooker Instructions: *Place all of the ingredients in a slow cooker and cook on low for 8 to 10 hours, until the onion and cabbage are very tender. Proceed with Step 3.*

Lower-Carb Modification:
Omit the honey.

GREAT WITH

Rye Bread

TOM YUM
(Thai hot and sour soup)

 YIELD: 4 to 6 servings | **PREP TIME:** 15 minutes | **STOVETOP:** 20 minutes

6 cups Chicken Broth (page 40), Dashi Broth (page 48), or Shrimp Cilantro Broth (page 54)

5 quarter-size slices fresh galangal or ginger, bruised

3 stalks lemongrass, bottom 3 inches only, halved lengthwise and bruised

¼ cup fresh lime juice

2 tablespoons fish sauce

2 tablespoons coconut sugar

1 tablespoon sambal oelek (ground chili paste)

½ medium onion, very thinly sliced

1 pound medium-large shrimp, peeled and deveined

4 ounces stemmed fresh enoki, white beech, or button mushrooms, or a combination

1 medium tomato, cut into 8 wedges

¼ cup fresh cilantro leaves, chopped

AIP Modification: *Use ginger instead of sambal oelek and omit the tomato.*

01 In a large pot, bring the broth to a boil with the galangal, lemongrass, lime juice, fish sauce, coconut sugar, and sambal oelek. Turn the heat down to medium-low and simmer, covered, for 15 minutes.

02 Remove and discard the lemongrass and galangal.

03 Turn the heat back up to high and add the onion, shrimp, and mushrooms. Cook for another 3 to 4 minutes, until the shrimp are cooked through. Turn off the heat and stir in the tomato and cilantro before serving.

TOM KA GAI
(Thai chicken coconut soup)

 YIELD: 4 to 6 servings | PREP TIME: 20 minutes | STOVETOP: 30 minutes

6 cups Chicken Broth (page 40)

1 stalk lemongrass, white part only, bruised with the dull side of a knife and chopped

1 bunch fresh cilantro, stems and leaves separated

2 serrano or Thai chiles or 1 jalapeño pepper, halved and seeded

1 (2-inch) piece fresh ginger, sliced into ¼-inch-thick rounds

3 fresh kaffir lime leaves or zest of ½ lime

1½ pounds boneless, skinless chicken thighs, cut into 1-inch pieces

1 pound shiitake, maitake, or oyster mushrooms (or a combination), stemmed and sliced

2 (14-ounce) cans full-fat coconut milk

2 tablespoons fish sauce

1 tablespoon coconut sugar

2 tablespoons chopped fresh cilantro leaves (from above)

Chili paste, for serving (optional)

01 In a large pot, combine the broth, lemongrass, cilantro stems, chiles, ginger, and lime leaves and bring to a simmer over medium-high heat. Cover, reduce the heat to low, and simmer for 20 minutes. Strain the broth through a fine-mesh strainer and discard the aromatics.

02 Add the chicken to the broth and cook for 5 minutes, or until just cooked through.

03 Add the mushrooms, coconut milk, fish sauce, and coconut sugar and cook for another 4 to 5 minutes, until the mushrooms are soft. Stir in the cilantro leaves.

04 Serve the soup with chili paste on the side for guests to add to their bowls, if desired.

> **Chef's Tip:** *To make straining easier, bundle the aromatics in cheesecloth or a mesh tea bag.*

AIP Modification: *Omit the serrano chiles and chili paste.*

Lower-Carb Modification:
Omit the coconut sugar.

CLASSIC BEEF PHO

 YIELD: 4 to 6 servings | **PREP TIME:** 10 minutes | **STOVETOP:** 5 minutes

3 to 4 quarts Pho Broth (page 56) (2 cups per serving)

1¼ pounds flank steak, sliced very thin

Sliced oxtail and beef shank from the pho broth

1 (6-inch) daikon, peeled and made into noodles with a julienne peeler or spiral slicer

1 to 2 green onions, sliced

Several sprigs fresh cilantro, mint, and/or Thai basil

1 to 2 serrano chiles or jalapeño peppers, sliced

6 to 8 cups cooked rice noodles, tapioca noodles, or zucchini noodles (page 194)

FOR SERVING:

Sriracha

Fish sauce

Lime wedges

01 Heat the broth until steaming.

02 Meanwhile, prepare a platter with the sliced flank steak, oxtail and beef shank, daikon noodles, green onions, fresh herbs, and chiles.

03 Divide the broth and noodles among four to six serving bowls.

04 Serve with the platter of steak and other ingredients to be added to the bowls of broth and noodles. Provide Sriracha, fish sauce, and lime wedges for people to add to their soup as they wish.

> **Chef's Tips:** *To make slicing easier, pop the flank steak in the freezer for 30 minutes. The steak will cook once it's added to the piping-hot broth.*
>
> *If you make the pho broth more than 3 days before making this soup, freeze the sliced oxtail and beef shank until needed.*

Lower-Carb Modification:
Use zucchini noodles instead of rice or tapioca noodles.

NEW ENGLAND CLAM CHOWDER

YIELD: 4 to 6 servings | PREP TIME: 20 minutes, plus time to cure | STOVETOP: 50 minutes

3 pounds cherrystone, quahog, or littleneck clams, well rinsed

4 ounces thick-cut bacon, cut into small dice

1 medium leek, white part only, cleaned and sliced into quarter-moons (about 1 cup) (see Tip on page 38)

1 cup diced shallots (about 2 large)

½ cup diced celery (about 2 ribs)

Pinch of salt

1 pound Yukon Gold potatoes, peeled and cut into small dice

½ teaspoon minced fresh thyme

½ cup white wine

1 tablespoon arrowroot starch

1 bay leaf

1 cup heavy cream, full-fat coconut milk, or Cashew Cream (page 58)

1 tablespoon minced fresh parsley, plus extra for garnish

01 In a large pot, bring 1 quart of water to a boil. Add the clams, cover, and cook for 5 to 10 minutes, until the clams open. Discard any clams that do not open. Transfer the clams to a rimmed baking sheet and set aside to cool. Strain the broth through a fine-mesh strainer lined with cheesecloth to catch any sediment. Reserve the broth.

02 Once the clams are cool enough to handle, remove them from their shells and chop them into small pieces. Set aside.

03 Rinse out the pot and return it to the stovetop over medium heat. Add the bacon and cook until crisp, about 10 minutes. Use a slotted spoon to remove the bacon to a plate. Remove all but 2 tablespoons of the fat from the pot.

04 Add the leek, shallots, and celery to the pot along with a pinch of salt and cook until softened, 7 to 8 minutes, stirring often.

05 Add the potatoes and thyme and cook for another 3 minutes. Turn the heat up to high and add the wine. Cook for another couple of minutes, until the liquid has mostly evaporated. Add the arrowroot starch and cook for 1 minute more, stirring constantly.

06 Pour in the reserved clam broth and add the bay leaf. Bring to a simmer and cook, partially covered, until the potatoes are tender, 15 to 20 minutes. Stir in the clams, cream, and half of the bacon and bring just to a simmer. Set aside at room temperature for up to an hour to allow the flavors to develop.

07 To serve, reheat the soup and stir in the parsley. Garnish with additional minced parsley and the remaining bacon.

Chef's Tip: *Rather not use wine? Swap the white wine for equal parts white wine vinegar and water.*

AIP Modification: *Use celery root, parsnips, or turnips instead of potatoes, and use coconut milk instead of heavy cream or cashew cream.*

Lower-Carb Modification: *Use celery root instead of potatoes.*

GREAT WITH

230   248

Oyster Crackers   Bread Bowls

MANHATTAN CLAM CHOWDER

YIELD: 4 to 6 servings | PREP TIME: 20 minutes, plus time to cure | STOVETOP: 40 minutes

3 pounds cherrystone, quahog, or littleneck clams, well rinsed

½ pound slab bacon or salt pork, cut into small dice

1 medium onion, cut into small dice

2 medium carrots, cut into small dice

2 celery ribs, cut into small dice

1 red, orange, or yellow bell pepper, cut into small dice

2 cloves garlic, minced

½ teaspoon red pepper flakes

3 sprigs fresh thyme

2 bay leaves

1 tablespoon tomato paste

1 (28-ounce) can whole tomatoes or 2 pounds fresh tomatoes (see page 21 for prep instructions)

1 large Yukon Gold potato, peeled and cut into small dice

¼ cup chopped fresh parsley

Salt and ground black pepper

01 In a large pot, bring 1 quart of water to a boil. Add the clams, cover, and cook for 5 to 10 minutes, until the clams open. Discard any clams that do not open. Transfer the clams to a rimmed baking sheet and set aside to cool. Strain the broth through a fine-mesh strainer lined with cheesecloth to catch any sediment. Reserve the broth.

02 Once the clams are cool enough to handle, remove them from their shells and chop them into small pieces. Set aside.

03 Rinse out the pot and return it to the stovetop over medium heat. Add the bacon and cook until some of the fat has rendered, about 5 minutes. Add the onion, carrots, celery, and bell pepper to the pot. Cook over medium heat for 8 to 10 minutes, until the vegetables have softened.

04 Add the garlic, red pepper flakes, thyme, bay leaves, and tomato paste. Cook for another minute, then add the tomatoes, potato, and clam broth. Bring to a simmer and cook, partially covered, until the chunks of potato are tender, 15 to 20 minutes.

05 Stir in the clams and parsley and remove the pot from the heat. Set aside at room temperature for up to an hour to allow the flavors to develop. Taste the broth and season with salt and pepper, if needed. Reheat before serving.

Lower-Carb Modification:
Use celery root instead of a potato.

GREAT WITH

Bread Bowls

ITALIAN WEDDING SOUP

 YIELD: 4 to 6 servings | PREP TIME: 15 minutes | STOVETOP: 10 minutes

FOR THE MEATBALLS:

1 large egg

2 tablespoons blanched almond flour

2 tablespoons minced fresh parsley

1 teaspoon minced fresh marjoram or oregano

1 clove garlic, grated or pressed

1 teaspoon salt

½ pound ground beef

½ pound ground pork

FOR THE SOUP:

1 tablespoon extra-virgin olive oil

1 small onion, minced

2 cloves garlic, minced

1 head escarole, chopped (about 6 cups)

2 quarts Chicken Broth (page 40)

2 large eggs

3 tablespoons grated Parmesan cheese (optional)

Lemon wedges, for serving (optional)

Red pepper flakes, for garnish (optional)

01 Make the meatballs: In a large bowl, mix together the egg, almond flour, parsley, marjoram, garlic, and salt. Add the beef and pork and mix with your hands until everything is well incorporated. Roll into small meatballs, about ¾ inch in diameter, and set aside.

02 In a large, heavy-bottomed pot, heat the olive oil over medium heat. When the oil is shimmering, add the onion and garlic. Cook for 4 to 5 minutes, until the onion is softened but not browned. Add the escarole and stir until it just starts to wilt. Turn up the heat, add the broth, and bring it to a low boil.

03 When the broth reaches a low boil, drop in the meatballs. Simmer until the meatballs are cooked through, 3 to 5 minutes.

04 While the meatballs are simmering, beat the eggs. Add the Parmesan to the eggs, if using.

05 When the meatballs are cooked, slowly pour the eggs into the soup, stirring as you pour.

06 Serve the soup with lemon wedges and garnished with red pepper flakes, if desired.

FRENCH ONION SOUP

YIELD: 6 servings | PREP TIME: 20 minutes
STOVETOP: 1 hour 30 minutes | SLOW COOKER: 18 to 20 hours | PRESSURE COOKER: 1 hour

1/4 cup ghee or avocado oil

2 tablespoons extra-virgin olive oil

3 pounds yellow onions, cut in half and thinly sliced

1 teaspoon coconut sugar

1 cup red wine

1 teaspoon minced fresh thyme

1 bay leaf

6 cups Roasted Vegetable Broth (page 36) or Basic Beef Broth (page 42)

12 diagonal slices Baguette (page 246), about 1 inch thick

6 ounces Gruyère cheese, shredded (about 1½ cups)

Chef's Tips: *The coconut sugar helps with the caramelization process, but it's fine to omit it if you are avoiding sugars.*

Rather not use wine? Swap the red wine for equal parts balsamic vinegar and water.

AIP Modification: *Use avocado oil instead of ghee. Omit the bread and cheese and use the wine modification above.*

Lower-Carb / Egg-Free Modification: *Omit the baguette.*

01 In a large heavy-bottomed pot, heat the ghee and olive oil over medium heat. When hot, stir in the onions, cover, and cook, stirring occasionally, for 10 minutes.

02 Remove the lid and stir in the coconut sugar. Reduce the heat to medium-low and cook, uncovered, for another 45 minutes to 1 hour, stirring occasionally. If the onions start to stick to the bottom at any point, turn down the heat. They should end up golden brown and caramelized, but only after cooking slowly for a long time.

03 Once the onions are caramelized, turn the heat up to high and pour in the wine. Cook for 2 to 3 minutes, until the alcohol smell is mostly gone. Add the thyme and bay leaf. Pour in the broth, bring the soup to a simmer, and simmer, uncovered, for 30 minutes.

04 While the soup is simmering, toast the bread: Preheat the oven to 350°F. Place the bread slices directly on the oven rack and toast for about 10 minutes per side.

05 To serve: Ladle the soup into six broiler-safe bowls. Place 2 toast slices in each bowl of soup and top with the Gruyère. Place the bowls under the broiler for 3 to 5 minutes, until the cheese is bubbly and just beginning to brown. If you don't have broiler-safe bowls, broil the cheese on the toasts and then float them on top of the soup.

 Slow Cooker Instructions: *Place the ghee, olive oil, onions, and coconut sugar in a slow cooker and stir to combine. Cook on low for 12 hours. After 12 hours, add the wine, thyme, bay leaf, and broth and cook for an additional 6 to 8 hours. Continue with Step 4.*

 Pressure Cooker Instructions: *Place the ghee, olive oil, onions, and coconut sugar in a pressure cooker and stir to combine. Set the pressure cooker to sauté (or put it over medium-high heat) and cook for 10 minutes, or until the onions start to release their liquid. Secure the lid and cook on high pressure for 15 minutes. Quick-release the pressure and remove the lid. Switch the cooker to sauté (or place it over medium-high heat) and continue with Step 3.*

MINESTRONE WITH ORECCHIETTE

 YIELD: 4 to 6 servings | PREP TIME: 15 minutes | STOVETOP: 20 minutes

8 ounces pancetta, diced

1 large onion, diced

3 medium carrots, diced

4 celery ribs, diced

4 cloves garlic, minced

1 quart Chicken Broth (page 40)

1 (28-ounce) can diced tomatoes or 2 pounds fresh tomatoes (see page 21 for prep instructions)

1 small celery root, peeled and diced

1 small cabbage, shredded

2 small summer squash or zucchini, diced

½ pound kale, stemmed and chopped

¼ pound green beans, cut into 1-inch pieces

1 batch cooked Orecchiette (page 198)

Chopped fresh basil leaves, for garnish

01 Heat a large pot over medium heat. When hot, add the pancetta. Cook for 4 to 5 minutes, stirring occasionally, until the pancetta is browned and the fat has rendered. With a slotted spoon, remove half of the pancetta and set aside to drain on paper towels, leaving the other half in the pot.

02 Add the onion, carrots, and celery. Cook for 6 to 8 minutes, until the onion is translucent. Add the garlic and cook for 1 minute more.

03 Add the broth, tomatoes, and celery root and bring to a simmer. Cook for 5 minutes, then add the cabbage, squash, kale, and green beans, bring to a simmer, and cook until the vegetables are tender, 5 to 6 minutes.

04 Add the orecchiette to heat through. Garnish with chopped basil and the reserved pancetta.

Lower-Carb / Egg-Free Modification: *Use veggie noodles (page 194) instead of Orecchiette.*

GREAT WITH

| Pesto | Rosemary-Garlic Oil | Baguette slices | Mini Boules |

SPICY SHRIMP AND CHORIZO SOUP

 YIELD: 4 to 6 servings | **PREP TIME:** 15 minutes | **STOVETOP:** 40 minutes

1 tablespoon plus 1 teaspoon avocado oil, divided

1 medium onion, cut into small dice

3 celery ribs, cut into small dice

1 red, orange, or yellow bell pepper, cut into small dice

4 cloves garlic, sliced

12 ounces Spanish-style dry-cured chorizo, cut into small dice, divided

1 tablespoon tomato paste

1½ teaspoons smoked paprika

1 teaspoon ground coriander

1 teaspoon salt

1 (28-ounce) can diced tomatoes or 2 pounds fresh tomatoes (see page 21 for prep instructions)

1 quart Shrimp Cilantro Broth (page 54) or Chicken Broth (page 40)

1 pound shrimp, peeled and deveined, and chopped

2 tablespoons minced fresh cilantro

1 avocado, diced or sliced, for serving

Chopped fresh cilantro, for garnish

01 Heat 1 tablespoon of the oil in a large, heavy-bottomed pot over medium-high heat. When the oil is shimmering, add the onion, celery, and bell pepper and cook, stirring occasionally, for 6 to 8 minutes, until the onion is translucent.

02 Add the garlic, three-quarters of the chorizo, tomato paste, smoked paprika, coriander, and salt and cook for 1 minute, stirring constantly, until very fragrant.

03 Add the tomatoes and cook for 5 minutes to cook the raw taste out.

04 Add the broth and bring to a simmer. Cook, uncovered, for 20 minutes.

05 Meanwhile, in a small sauté pan, heat the remaining teaspoon of oil over high heat. When the oil is hot, add the remaining chorizo and cook for 5 minutes, or until crispy. Set aside to drain on paper towels.

06 Taste the soup and add additional smoked paprika, coriander, and salt if needed. Add the shrimp and simmer until just cooked through, 3 to 4 minutes. Remove from the heat, stir in the minced cilantro, and serve topped with the crispy chorizo, avocado, and chopped cilantro.

MEAT AND POTATOES SOUP

 YIELD: 4 to 6 servings | **PREP TIME:** 10 minutes | **STOVETOP:** 25 minutes

1 pound ground beef

3 celery ribs, cut into small dice

1 small onion, cut into small dice

4 cloves garlic, minced

2 tablespoons tomato paste

3 cups Basic Beef Broth (page 42)

1 (14-ounce) can diced tomatoes or 1 pound fresh tomatoes (see page 21 for prep instructions)

3 medium carrots, cut into small dice

1 pound Yukon Gold or russet potatoes, peeled and cut into ½-inch pieces

1 teaspoon salt

½ teaspoon dried oregano leaves

½ teaspoon smoked paprika

⅛ teaspoon cayenne pepper

Minced fresh parsley or chives, for garnish (optional)

01 In a large heavy-bottomed pot over medium-high heat, sauté the beef, celery, and onion, stirring occasionally to break up the meat, for 5 minutes, or until some of the fat has rendered.

02 Tilt the pot and scoop out most of the fat, leaving about 1 tablespoon in the pot. Add the garlic and tomato paste and cook for 2 minutes, stirring often.

03 Add the broth, tomatoes, carrots, potatoes, salt, oregano, smoked paprika, and cayenne pepper. Bring to a simmer and cook for 15 to 20 minutes, until the potatoes and carrots are tender.

04 Garnish the bowls of soup with parsley or chives, if desired.

Lower-Carb Modification:
Use celery root instead of potatoes.

GREAT WITH

Pull-Apart Dinner Rolls

CALDO VERDE
(Portuguese potato soup)

 YIELD: 4 to 6 servings | **PREP TIME:** 20 minutes | **STOVETOP:** 35 minutes

1 tablespoon avocado oil or lard

1 pound linguiça sausage, removed from casings and broken into small chunks (see Tip)

1 large red onion, cut into small dice

6 cloves garlic, minced

6 medium russet potatoes, peeled and diced

2 quarts Chicken Broth (page 40)

1 bunch collards (about ¾ pound), stemmed and sliced very thinly

Chef's Tip: *If you can't find linguiça, you can substitute Spanish-style dry-cured chorizo.*

01 In a large heavy-bottomed pot, heat the oil over medium-high heat. When the oil is hot, add the sausage and cook until browned and cooked through, about 5 minutes. Using a slotted spoon, remove the sausage to a bowl and set aside.

02 Add the onion to the pot and cook until golden brown and softened, 4 to 5 minutes. Add the garlic and cook for 1 minute.

03 Add the potatoes, broth, and half of the cooked sausage to the pot and bring to a boil. Turn down the heat and simmer for 10 to 15 minutes, until the potatoes are softened.

04 Puree half of the soup in a blender, then return it to the pot. Alternatively, you can use an immersion blender to coarsely puree the soup right in the pot. Add the collards and cook for 10 minutes, or until they are softened.

05 Serve topped with the remaining linguiça.

HOT AND SOUR SOUP

 YIELD: 4 to 6 servings | **PREP TIME:** 15 minutes | **STOVETOP:** 35 minutes

½ cup dried Chinese black mushrooms

24 dried lily buds, tough ends cut off and quartered lengthwise

2 quarts Pork Broth with Shiitake Mushrooms and Ginger (page 46) or Chicken Broth (page 40)

1 (4-by-6-inch) piece kombu, rinsed

1 (2-inch) piece fresh ginger, peeled and grated

1 teaspoon ground white pepper

¼ cup coconut aminos

¼ cup coconut vinegar or unseasoned rice vinegar

2 tablespoons arrowroot starch

2 large eggs, beaten

1 tablespoon toasted sesame oil

½ cup sliced green onions, for garnish

Chili oil, for drizzling (optional)

01 Place the dried mushrooms and lily buds in a large bowl, cover with boiling water, and set aside to reconstitute. When the mushrooms are soft enough to cut, drain the liquid and slice the mushrooms thinly.

02 Heat the broth in a large soup pot over medium heat. Add the rinsed kombu and grated ginger and simmer for 20 to 25 minutes. Remove and discard the kombu.

03 Add the rehydrated mushrooms and lily buds, white pepper, coconut aminos, and vinegar and simmer for 5 minutes.

04 In a small bowl, whisk the arrowroot starch with ¼ cup of cool water to create a slurry. Stir the slurry into the soup and simmer for an additional 5 minutes.

05 While stirring, slowly pour in the beaten eggs.

06 Add the toasted sesame oil and turn off the heat.

07 Serve garnished with sliced green onions and a drizzle of chili oil, if desired.

Chef's Tip: *Chinese black mushrooms, dried lily buds, and kombu can be found at Asian markets.*

Egg-Free Modification: *Omit the eggs.*

TUSCAN TOMATO SOUP

 YIELD: 6 servings | **PREP TIME:** 15 minutes | **STOVETOP:** 45 minutes

2 (28-ounce) cans whole tomatoes or 4 pounds fresh tomatoes (see page 21 for prep instructions)

2 tablespoons extra-virgin olive oil

1 medium onion, cut into small dice

2 medium carrots, cut into small dice

2 celery ribs, cut into small dice

1 teaspoon salt

4 cloves garlic, minced

1 teaspoon minced fresh rosemary

1 tablespoon tomato paste

1 bay leaf

5 cloves roasted garlic (see Tip)

2 cups Chicken Broth (page 40) or Veggie-Herb Broth (page 38)

1 tablespoon balsamic vinegar

2 tablespoons Rosemary-Garlic Oil (page 208), plus 2 to 4 tablespoons for drizzling

01 Crush the tomatoes with your hands so you have a loose puree.

02 Heat the olive oil in a large pot over medium-high heat. When the oil is hot, add the onion, carrots, celery, and salt. Sauté for 10 to 12 minutes, until the veggies are softened, stirring occasionally.

03 Add the garlic and rosemary and cook for another minute, then stir in the tomato paste. Add the crushed tomatoes, bay leaf, roasted garlic, and broth and bring to a simmer. Cover, turn the heat down to medium-low, and cook for 20 minutes. Remove the lid and stir in the balsamic vinegar. Turn up the heat to medium-high and simmer, uncovered, for an additional 10 minutes.

04 Coarsely blend the soup. You can puree half in a blender and then return the puree to the pot (for a half-smooth, half-chunky texture), or you can use an immersion blender. Stir in 2 tablespoons of the Rosemary-Garlic Oil.

05 Drizzle each bowl with 1 to 2 teaspoons of the Rosemary-Garlic Oil before serving.

> **Chef's Tip:** *If you saved the garlic after making Rosemary-Garlic Oil, you can use it in this recipe. If not, break up a bulb of garlic into cloves and toss them with enough olive oil to coat. Roast on a rimmed baking sheet at 375°F for about 30 minutes, until the garlic is tender. Once cool enough to handle, squeeze the cloves out of their skins. You'll have more than you need for this recipe, but you will find that it makes a wonderful addition to many recipes!*

GREAT WITH

Cauliflower Rice   *Orecchiette*   *Breadsticks*

MATZO BALL SOUP

 YIELD: 4 to 6 servings | **PREP TIME:** 15 minutes | **STOVETOP:** 12 minutes

2 large carrots, cut into small dice

2 small parsnips, peeled and cut into small dice

3 celery ribs, cut into ¼-inch slices

6 cups Chicken Broth (page 40)

2 cups diced cooked chicken

1 batch cooked Matzo Balls (page 190)

1 tablespoon minced fresh dill

1 tablespoon minced fresh parsley

Salt and ground black pepper

01 Place the carrots, parsnips, celery, and chicken broth in a large pot. Bring to a boil and cook, partially covered, for 10 minutes, or until the vegetables are tender.

02 Add the chicken and matzo balls and cook for another 2 minutes, or until just heated through.

03 Stir in the dill and parsley. Season to taste with salt and pepper and serve.

VIETNAMESE CRAB AND ASPARAGUS SOUP

 YIELD: 4 to 6 servings | **PREP TIME:** 10 minutes | **STOVETOP:** 10 minutes

1 tablespoon avocado oil

1 cup sliced shallots (about 2 large)

½ teaspoon salt

1 pound asparagus, woody ends trimmed, sliced on the bias into 1-inch pieces

2 cloves garlic, minced or grated

1 teaspoon grated fresh ginger

6 cups Shrimp Cilantro Broth (page 54) or Chicken Broth (page 40)

2 teaspoons tapioca starch, divided

1 large egg, well beaten

1 pound crab meat

Ground white pepper, for serving (optional)

Toasted sesame oil, for serving (optional)

01 Heat the avocado oil in a large heavy-bottomed pot over medium heat. When the oil is shimmering, add the shallots and salt and cook for 4 to 5 minutes, until softened.

02 Add the asparagus, garlic, and ginger and cook for 1 minute, or until fragrant. Add the broth and bring to a boil.

03 In a small bowl, combine 1 teaspoon of the tapioca starch with 2 teaspoons of cool water to create a slurry. Stir the slurry into the soup and cook for 2 minutes, until thickened slightly.

04 Meanwhile, combine the remaining teaspoon of tapioca starch with the egg and beat well to combine. Pour the egg mixture into the soup while stirring.

05 Stir in the crab meat and cook for another minute, until just heated through.

06 Season the bowls of soup with a dash of white pepper and/or sesame oil, if desired.

AIP Modification: *Omit the egg, white pepper, and toasted sesame oil.*

Egg-Free Modification: *Omit the egg.*

EGG DROP SOUP

 YIELD: 4 to 6 servings | PREP TIME: 5 minutes | STOVETOP: 15 minutes

2 quarts Chicken Broth
(page 40)

1 stalk lemongrass, bruised
with the back of a knife and cut
into 4 pieces

2 whole star anise

1 cinnamon stick

6 quarter-size slices fresh
ginger

1 tablespoon coconut aminos

1 teaspoon fish sauce

Salt

2 tablespoons plus 2 teaspoons
tapioca starch, divided

4 large eggs

1 teaspoon toasted sesame oil

1 to 2 chives (preferably garlic
chives), thinly sliced on the
bias, for garnish (optional)

01 Combine the broth, lemongrass, star anise, cinnamon stick, and ginger in a large pot. Bring to a simmer and cover. Turn the heat down to low and cook for 10 to 15 minutes, until the broth is very fragrant. Remove the aromatics.

02 Stir in the coconut aminos and fish sauce and taste the broth. Season to taste with salt, and add more coconut aminos or fish sauce, if needed.

03 Remove a ladleful of broth to a small bowl and whisk in 2 tablespoons of the tapioca starch to create a slurry. Stir the slurry into the soup.

04 In a small bowl, whisk the eggs with the remaining 2 teaspoons of tapioca starch. Adjust the heat under the soup so the soup is barely simmering. Hold a fork over the pot and pour the eggs through the tines of the fork into the soup, mixing gently as you go. Turn off the heat and stir in the sesame oil. Serve garnished with chives, if desired.

BUILD YOUR OWN RAMEN

 The fun thing about ramen is that there are virtually endless ways to make it; creating your perfect bowl is half the fun! Pick a broth, pick a noodle, and serve with as many filling and topping options as you'd like.

BROTH
(about 6 ounces per serving)

Chicken Broth (page 40)

Basic Beef Broth (page 42)

Roasted Beef and Mushroom Broth (page 44)

Pork Broth with Shiitake Mushrooms and Ginger (page 46)

Dashi Broth (page 48)

Shrimp Cilantro Broth (page 54)

+ NOODLES

Homemade Noodles (page 198)
(omit for AIP, lower-carb, and egg-free)

Veggie Noodles (page 194)

+ PROTEIN
(3 to 4 ounces per serving)

Cooked Wrapper-Less Wontons (page 200)

Thinly sliced flank steak

Shredded rotisserie chicken

Cooked shrimp

Soft-boiled egg *(omit for AIP and egg-free)*

+ EXTRAS
(a tablespoon or two per serving)

Pea shoots

Kimchi *(omit for AIP)*

Fresh Thai basil leaves

Fresh mint leaves

Fresh cilantro leaves

Sliced green onions

Sliced garlic chives

+ EXTRA FLAVORINGS

Sriracha or chili paste *(omit for AIP)*

Fish sauce

Coconut aminos

Toasted sesame oil *(omit for AIP)*

Coconut milk *(for a creamy broth)*

CHICKEN TORTILLA SOUP

YIELD: 4 to 6 servings | PREP TIME: 15 minutes | STOVETOP: 50 minutes (not including time to roast peppers)

2 red, orange, or yellow bell peppers

1 tablespoon lard or avocado oil

1 whole bone-in, skin-on chicken breast

1 medium onion, cut into small dice

4 cloves garlic, sliced

2 teaspoons smoked paprika

1 teaspoon ground coriander

1 teaspoon ground cumin

1 teaspoon salt

½ teaspoon chipotle powder

1 (14-ounce) can diced tomatoes or 1 pound fresh tomatoes (see page 21 for prep instructions)

6 cups Chicken Broth (page 40)

FOR SERVING:

1 lime, quartered

2 avocados, diced

Chopped fresh cilantro

Crispy Tortilla Strips (page 232)

Lower-Carb Modification:
Omit the Crispy Tortilla Strips. To add some crunch, use julienned jicama or daikon.

01   Roast the peppers following one of the methods below. Cut them into a small dice and set aside.

02   Heat the lard in a large pot over medium-high heat. Place the chicken breast skin side down in the pan and cook for about 5 minutes on each side, until browned. Remove to a plate.

03   Add the onion to the pot and sauté, stirring occasionally, for 8 to 10 minutes, until softened and browned. Add the garlic and cook for 1 more minute.

04   Add the smoked paprika, coriander, cumin, salt, and chipotle powder and cook for another 30 seconds, stirring constantly.

05   Add the tomatoes, broth, roasted peppers, and chicken and bring to a boil. Turn the heat down to medium-low and simmer, uncovered, for 25 to 30 minutes.

06   Remove the chicken and remove and discard the skin and bones. Shred the meat with two forks and return it to the pot.

07   To serve, garnish each bowl of soup with a lime wedge, chopped avocado, cilantro leaves, and tortilla chips.

To roast the peppers over a gas flame: *Turn the burner to medium-high and place the peppers directly on the grate above the burner. Allow the peppers to blister and blacken before turning them with tongs to blacken them on all sides. Remove the peppers to a heatproof bowl and cover with plastic wrap.*

To roast the peppers in the oven: *Place an oven rack in the top position and turn the broiler to high. Place the peppers on a rimmed baking sheet and broil for 25 to 30 minutes, turning every 5 minutes or so, until they are blackened on all sides. Remove to a heatproof bowl and cover with plastic wrap.*

After the peppers have steamed in the bowl for 15 minutes, remove them and rub off the skins. Although it's tempting to run the peppers under water, doing so would remove a lot of the smoky flavor from the roasting, so try to be patient and peel them without using water.

CHICKEN AND DUMPLINGS SOUP

YIELD: 6 servings | PREP TIME: 35 minutes | STOVETOP: 45 minutes | SLOW COOKER: 9 to 11 hours

½ cup arrowroot starch

1 teaspoon salt

½ teaspoon ground black pepper

1 whole chicken, cut into 8 pieces

2 tablespoons ghee

1 medium onion, cut into small dice

2 celery ribs, cut into small dice

2 medium carrots, cut into small dice

½ teaspoon minced fresh thyme

¼ teaspoon turmeric powder

2 quarts Chicken Broth (page 40)

¾ cup full-fat coconut milk

FOR THE DUMPLINGS:

¾ cup blanched almond flour

¾ cup cassava flour

¾ teaspoon baking soda

1½ teaspoons salt

¾ cup full-fat coconut milk

Chopped fresh parsley or chives, for garnish (optional)

01 In a large bowl, whisk together the arrowroot starch, salt, and pepper. Dredge the chicken pieces in the mixture, coating them on all sides.

02 In a large heavy-bottomed pot, heat the ghee. When hot, add the chicken in batches and cook until golden brown on all sides, 4 to 5 minutes per side.

03 Remove the chicken and set aside. Add the onion, celery, and carrots to the pot and sauté for 5 to 7 minutes, until the veggies have softened.

04 Stir the thyme and turmeric into the vegetables. Pour in the broth, scraping up any browned bits that are stuck to the bottom of the pot.

05 Return the chicken to the pot and bring to a simmer. Simmer the soup until the chicken is cooked through, about 20 minutes. Remove the chicken pieces and set them aside to cool.

06 While the soup is simmering, make the dumplings: Mix together the almond flour, cassava flour, baking soda, salt, and coconut milk. Use your hands to form the dough into 24 small dumplings. The dumplings should be somewhat round but still rustic looking.

07 Drop the dumplings into the simmering soup and cook for 5 minutes.

08 When the chicken is cool enough to handle, remove the meat from the bones and shred it. Discard the skin and bones. (Save the bones for making broth, if desired.)

09 Add the shredded chicken and coconut milk to the soup and simmer for another 3 to 4 minutes, until heated through. Garnish with fresh parsley or chives, if desired.

 Slow Cooker Instructions: *After completing Step 4, transfer the contents of the pot to a slow cooker and add the chicken. Cook on low for 8 to 10 hours, until the chicken is cooked through. Remove the chicken pieces from the pot and allow to cool. Complete Step 6, then turn the heat up to high and add the dumplings to the slow cooker, allowing them to cook for 20 minutes, or until they're cooked through. Proceed with Steps 8 and 9, cooking the soup for about 10 minutes to heat through.*

BEEF BORSCHT

YIELD: 4 to 6 servings | PREP TIME: 20 minutes | STOVETOP: 1 hour 30 minutes
SLOW COOKER: 8 hours 45 minutes to 10 hours 45 minutes | PRESSURE COOKER: 1 hour 15 minutes

¼ cup arrowroot starch

1 teaspoon salt

½ teaspoon ground black pepper

2 pounds boneless beef chuck, cut into ½-inch to ¾-inch cubes

2 tablespoons avocado oil or light olive oil, divided

1 extra-large onion, diced

4 medium carrots, diced

3 celery ribs, diced

6 cloves garlic, chopped

2 tablespoons tomato paste

2 (28-ounce) cans whole peeled tomatoes or 4 pounds fresh tomatoes (see page 21 for prep instructions)

2 quarts Basic Beef Broth (page 42)

3 medium turnips, peeled and diced (about 3 cups)

½ medium head cabbage, shredded (about 4 cups)

4 large beets, peeled and cut into matchsticks

3 tablespoons red wine vinegar

1 tablespoon minced fresh dill, plus more for garnish

Dairy-Free Sour Cream (page 62), for serving

Nut-Free Modification: *Omit the dairy-free sour cream.*

01 In a large bowl, whisk together the arrowroot starch, salt, and pepper. Add the beef and toss to coat well.

02 In a large pot, heat 1 tablespoon of the oil over high heat. When the oil is hot, add half of the beef and cook until browned on all sides, about 5 minutes. Remove the meat to a bowl. Repeat with the remaining tablespoon of oil and beef.

03 Add the onion, carrots, and celery to the pot and cook for about 10 minutes, until the onions are translucent. Add the garlic and tomato paste and cook for 1 more minute.

04 Lightly crush the tomatoes with your hands; add the crushed tomatoes, their juices, and the broth to the pot, along with the browned beef. Bring to a simmer and cover. Turn the heat down to low so the soup is at a bare simmer and cook for 30 minutes, or until the beef is almost tender.

05 Add the turnips and cabbage and cook for 15 minutes.

06 Add the beets, vinegar, and dill and cook for another 30 minutes, until all of the veggies are tender.

07 Serve the soup with a dollop of sour cream, sprinkled with fresh dill.

 Slow Cooker Instructions: *After completing Step 1, place the beef, onion, carrots, celery, garlic, tomato paste, crushed tomatoes and juices, broth, turnips, and cabbage in a slow cooker and cook on low for 8 to 10 hours, until the beef is almost tender. Add the beets, vinegar, and dill, then turn the slow cooker up to high and cook, uncovered, for 45 minutes, until the beets are tender.*

 Pressure Cooker Instructions: *After completing Step 1, place the beef, onion, carrots, celery, garlic, tomato paste, crushed tomatoes and juices, broth, turnips, and cabbage in a pressure cooker. Secure the lid and cook for 35 minutes on high pressure. Allow the pressure to release naturally for 10 minutes before opening the lid. Switch to the sauté function and add the beets, vinegar, and dill. Cook, uncovered, for 30 to 45 minutes, until all of the veggies are tender.*

BURMESE CHICKEN NOODLE SOUP

 YIELD: 4 to 6 servings | **PREP TIME:** 20 minutes | **STOVETOP:** 45 minutes

1¼ pounds boneless, skinless chicken thighs, cut into 1-inch pieces

2 tablespoons fish sauce

1 tablespoon coconut sugar

2 teaspoons paprika

2 teaspoons turmeric powder

½ teaspoon cayenne pepper

1 tablespoon coconut oil

2 medium onions, thinly sliced

Pinch of salt

6 cups Chicken Broth (page 40)

2 (14-ounce) cans full-fat coconut milk

2 tablespoons tapioca starch

1 batch cooked Homemade Noodles (page 198) or 8 ounces cooked tapioca noodles

4 to 6 hard-boiled eggs (1 per serving), sliced, for garnish

Chopped fresh cilantro, for garnish

6 lemon wedges, for serving

01 In a medium bowl, toss the chicken, fish sauce, coconut sugar, paprika, turmeric, and cayenne pepper until the chicken is evenly coated. Set aside.

02 Heat the coconut oil in a large heavy-bottomed pot over medium-high heat. When the oil is shimmering, add the onions. Cook, stirring occasionally, until golden brown, 7 to 8 minutes. Reduce the heat to medium-low, add a pinch of salt, and cook for another 5 to 6 minutes, until the onions are soft.

03 Add the coated chicken and any marinade that's left in the bowl to the pot with the onions and turn the heat up to medium-high. Cook until the chicken is just cooked through, 4 to 5 minutes.

04 Add the broth and coconut milk. Bring to a simmer and cook for 20 minutes. In a small bowl, mix ½ cup of the hot soup broth with the tapioca starch to create a slurry. Stir the slurry into the soup and simmer for an additional 3 to 5 minutes, until thickened slightly.

05 Divide the noodles among serving bowls and pour in a ladleful of the soup. Top each bowl with a sliced hard-boiled egg and some chopped cilantro, and serve with a lemon wedge on the side.

AIP Modification: *Omit the paprika and cayenne pepper, add 2 teaspoons of peeled and grated fresh ginger, and use veggie noodles (page 194) instead of Homemade Noodles or tapioca noodles.*

Lower-Carb Modification: *Omit the coconut sugar and use veggie noodles (page 194) instead of Homemade Noodles or tapioca noodles.*

Egg-Free Modification: *Omit the hard-boiled eggs and use tapioca noodles instead of Homemade Noodles.*

LOBSTER BISQUE

YIELD: 4 servings | PREP TIME: 20 minutes, plus time to chill the lobsters | STOVETOP: about 1 hour 15 minutes
SLOW COOKER: 6 hours 30 minutes to 8 hours 30 minutes | PRESSURE COOKER: 40 minutes

2 (1- to 1½-pound) live lobsters (see Tip)

3 tablespoons unsalted butter, ghee, or avocado oil

3 tablespoons extra-virgin olive oil

1 cup diced shallots (about 2 large)

1 cup diced carrots (about 2 medium)

1 cup diced celery (about 4 ribs)

2 cloves garlic, roughly chopped

2 tablespoons tomato paste

2 (2-inch) strips orange zest

1 bay leaf

1 sprig fresh thyme

½ cup cognac

3 tablespoons arrowroot starch

2 cups Fish Broth (page 52), Chicken Broth (page 40), or Veggie-Herb Broth (page 38), or more if using steamed lobsters (see Tip)

2 cups heavy cream or full-fat coconut milk

½ teaspoon minced fresh tarragon

Chef's Tip: *If you'd prefer to skip Steps 1 through 3, purchase steamed lobsters from your fishmonger. Use extra broth in place of the reserved cooking liquid.*

01 Bring a large pot of water to a boil.

02 Place the lobsters in the freezer for 20 to 30 minutes. Remove a lobster from the freezer and place it on its back on a large rimmed cutting board or on a flat cutting board nested inside a rimmed baking sheet. Insert a chef's knife directly behind where the claws attach to the body; with a swift motion, cut toward the head. Repeat with the second lobster.

03 Carefully plunge the lobsters into the boiling water and cover the pot. Boil for 10 minutes. Remove the lobsters and allow them to cool slightly on a cutting board. Reserve 1 quart of the cooking liquid.

04 Remove the meat from the lobsters: Tear off the claws and tail. Working over a bowl to catch the juices, use a shell cracker to break open the claws, then pull out the meat. Cut the tail lengthwise through the underside and pull out the meat. Cut the meat into small pieces. Reserve the shells and bodies in a bowl.

05 In a large heavy-bottomed pot, heat the butter and olive oil over medium-high heat. Add the shallots, carrots, celery, garlic, tomato paste, orange zest, bay leaf, and thyme and stir them into the fat, then add the lobster shells, bodies, and any juices that are in the bowl. Cook for about 10 minutes, stirring often, until the vegetables are soft.

06 Turn the heat up to high and add the cognac. Cook for 2 to 3 minutes, until the liquid is almost gone. Stir in the arrowroot starch and cook for another 2 minutes.

07 Add the reserved cooking liquid, fish broth, and cream and bring to a boil. As soon as it comes to a boil, turn the heat down to a bare simmer. Cook for 45 minutes to 1 hour, until the soup is reduced and thickened.

08 Strain the solids out of the soup through a fine-mesh strainer, pressing out all of the liquid with a wooden spoon.

09 Rinse out the pot and return the liquid to it. Add the reserved lobster meat and tarragon and cook until just heated through, about 2 minutes.

Slow Cooker Instructions:
After completing Step 6, transfer the contents of the pot to a slow cooker and add 3 cups of the reserved cooking liquid, 1 cup of fish broth, and the cream. Cook on low for 6 to 8 hours. Continue with Step 8.

Pressure Cooker Instructions: *After completing Step 6, transfer the contents of the pot to a pressure cooker and add 3 cups of the reserved cooking liquid, 1 cup of fish broth, and the cream. Secure the lid and cook on high pressure for 15 minutes, then allow the pressure to release naturally before opening the lid. Continue with Step 8.*

OXTAIL AND SMOKED PORK GUMBO
with spicy roasted okra

YIELD: 4 to 6 servings | PREP TIME: 10 minutes | STOVETOP: 4 hours

2½ pounds oxtail

1¾ teaspoons salt, divided

½ teaspoon ground black pepper

¼ cup plus 1 tablespoon avocado oil or light olive oil, divided

1 medium yellow onion, cut into small dice

2 celery ribs, cut into small dice

1 red bell pepper, cut into small dice

4 cloves garlic, minced

3 tablespoons arrowroot starch

2 teaspoons paprika

1 teaspoon red pepper flakes

¾ teaspoon dried oregano leaves

½ teaspoon granulated garlic

¼ teaspoon cayenne pepper

1 quart Chicken Broth (page 40)

¾ pound smoked pulled pork shank or hock meat (from 1 smoked pork shank, about 2 pounds, or 2 smoked ham hocks)

12 ounces andouille sausage, sliced thin

1 bunch green onions, sliced (reserve the tops for garnish)

1 batch Spicy Roasted Okra (page 250), for serving

01 Season the oxtail with 1 teaspoon of the salt and the pepper.

02 In a large, heavy-bottomed pot, heat 1 tablespoon of the oil over medium-high heat. When the oil is hot, add the oxtail and cook until browned on all sides, about 15 minutes. Remove to a plate.

03 Pour off the rendered fat from the oxtail and add the remaining ¼ cup of oil to the pot. Add the onion, celery, and bell pepper and sauté over medium-high heat, stirring occasionally, until softened and starting to brown, about 8 minutes. Add the garlic and sauté for another minute.

04 Add the arrowroot starch and reduce the heat to medium. Cook for 5 minutes, stirring often. The mixture will start to get sticky, but don't worry; adding the broth will fix that.

05 Add the spices, broth, and remaining ¾ teaspoon of salt, scraping up any browned bits that are stuck to the bottom of the pan. Turn the heat up to high and bring to a boil. Cook, uncovered, for 5 minutes.

06 Add the oxtail and pork shank and turn the heat down to medium-low. Cover and simmer for 3 hours, or until the oxtail is tender. Skim as much of the fat off the top as possible.

07 Add the sausage and green onions and bring the soup to a low boil. Cook for another 20 to 30 minutes, until the soup has thickened.

08 Garnish with green onion tops and serve with Spicy Roasted Okra.

GREAT WITH

Cauliflower Rice   Drop Biscuits

WEST AFRICAN CASHEW SOUP

 YIELD: 4 to 6 servings | **PREP TIME:** 15 minutes | **STOVETOP:** 30 minutes

3 tablespoons light olive oil or avocado oil, divided

½ cup raw cashews, chopped

1 large onion, cut into small dice

2 tablespoons peeled and grated fresh ginger

1½ pounds boneless, skinless chicken thighs

1 teaspoon salt

1 teaspoon ancho chili powder

1 teaspoon cayenne pepper

1 teaspoon ground coriander

1 teaspoon turmeric powder

½ teaspoon ground cumin

½ teaspoon fenugreek seeds

1 (14-ounce) can diced tomatoes or 1 pound fresh tomatoes (see page 21 for prep instructions)

2 tablespoons tomato paste

1 pound sweet potatoes (about 2 medium), peeled and cut into small dice

1 bunch kale (about ½ pound), stemmed and cut into 1-inch pieces

6 to 8 cups Chicken Broth (page 40)

½ cup roasted, unsalted cashew butter

01 Heat 2 tablespoons of the oil in a large soup pot over medium heat. When the oil is hot, add the cashews and cook, stirring constantly, for 2 to 3 minutes, until toasted and fragrant. Remove the cashews with a slotted spoon and set aside.

02 Add the onion and cook, stirring often, for about 5 minutes, until golden brown and softened. Add the ginger and cook for another minute, stirring constantly.

03 Add the remaining tablespoon of oil to the pot, then add the chicken. Cook until the chicken is opaque on all sides, about 5 minutes.

04 Stir in the salt and spices and cook for another minute, stirring constantly. Add the diced tomatoes, tomato paste, sweet potatoes, kale, and 6 cups of the broth. Bring to a simmer and cook until the sweet potatoes are tender and the chicken is cooked through, about 10 minutes.

05 Stir in the cashew butter and cook for 2 to 3 more minutes, until the soup has thickened. Add up to 2 cups more broth if you prefer a thinner soup.

06 Serve garnished with the toasted cashews.

CHAPTER 4:

STEWS AND CHILIS

I haven't done any scientific research on this, but I'm willing to bet that when "Brrrrr!" starts being uttered is right around the time people start making stews and chilis. There is nothing more warming and comforting than tucking into a bowl of stick-to-your-ribs stew after coming in from the cold.

Most of the recipes in this chapter are just that: hearty and comforting. But that doesn't mean you have to skip this chapter in the warmer months! A few of these recipes—like San Francisco Cioppino (page 154) and Brazilian Fish Stew (page 152)—are quick to make and still light, despite being stews.

There is lots of room for creativity in this chapter. The proteins can be swapped in just about all of these recipes. For example, if you love the flavors of the Spicy Lamb Curry (page 158) but have beef that needs to be cooked, use the beef instead. Chicken works great with the flavors of the Roasted Tomatillo Pork Chili Verde (page 164), and if you're in a hurry, you can use ground chicken thighs in the White Chicken Chili (page 166).

To make life easier, I've included slow cooker and pressure cooker instructions for as many long-cooking recipes (those that take longer than 45 minutes to cook on the stovetop) as possible.

FIVE-SPICE BEEF STEW
with sweet potatoes and baby bok choy

YIELD: 4 to 6 servings | PREP TIME: 15 minutes | STOVETOP: 2 hours 30 minutes
SLOW COOKER: 8 hours 30 minutes to 10 hours 30 minutes | PRESSURE COOKER: 40 minutes

1 tablespoon avocado oil or coconut oil

1 large onion, sliced

4 cloves garlic, sliced

1 (1-inch) piece fresh ginger, peeled and grated

½ teaspoon Chinese five-spice powder

2 cups Basic Beef Broth (page 42), Chicken Broth (page 40), or water

½ cup dry sherry or rice wine

¼ cup coconut aminos

3 pounds beef stew meat or beef chuck, cut into 1-inch pieces

2 teaspoons salt

½ teaspoon ground black pepper

1 tablespoon tapioca starch

1½ pounds sweet potatoes, peeled and chopped

½ pound baby bok choy, halved

1 teaspoon fish sauce

3 to 4 green onions, sliced on the diagonal, for garnish

01 In a large, heavy-bottomed pot with a lid, heat the oil over medium-high heat. When the oil is shimmering, add the onion and sauté until nicely browned, 5 to 6 minutes. Add the garlic, ginger, and Chinese five-spice and sauté for another 30 seconds, until fragrant.

02 Add the broth, sherry, and coconut aminos and bring to a boil. Season the beef with the salt and pepper and add it to the pot. Reduce the heat to low so that the liquid is just barely simmering. Cover and cook for 1½ to 2 hours, until the beef is fork-tender.

03 In a small bowl, whisk together the tapioca starch with 1 cup of the stew liquid to create a slurry. Pour the slurry into the stew and stir.

04 Add the sweet potatoes and simmer for another 20 minutes, or until the potatoes are tender.

05 Add the bok choy and fish sauce and cook for another 5 minutes, until the bok choy is tender.

06 Serve the stew garnished with sliced green onions.

 Slow Cooker Instructions: *After completing Step 1, transfer the contents of the pot to a slow cooker. Season the beef with the salt and pepper and add it to the slow cooker, along with the broth, sherry, coconut aminos, and sweet potatoes. Cook on low for 8 to 10 hours, until the beef is fork-tender. Turn the heat up to high and complete Step 3, then proceed with Step 5.*

 Pressure Cooker Instructions: *After completing Step 1, transfer the contents of the pot to a pressure cooker. Season the beef with the salt and pepper and add it to the slow cooker, along with the broth, sherry, coconut aminos, and sweet potatoes. Secure the lid and cook at high pressure for 30 minutes. Quick-release the pressure and open the lid. Switch to the sauté function and complete Step 3, then proceed with Step 5.*

BRAZILIAN FISH STEW

 YIELD: 4 to 6 servings | **PREP TIME:** 10 minutes, plus 30 minutes to marinate | **STOVETOP:** 30 minutes

1 teaspoon finely grated lemon zest, divided

1 teaspoon finely grated lime zest, divided

¼ cup fresh lemon juice

¼ cup fresh lime juice

4 tablespoons chopped fresh cilantro, divided

1 pound firm, mild white fish fillets, such as cod, snapper, or halibut, cut into ½- to ¾-inch pieces

1 pound large shrimp, peeled and deveined

1 tablespoon coconut oil

1 large onion, sliced

2 cloves garlic, minced

1 (14-ounce) can diced tomatoes or 1 pound fresh tomatoes (see page 21 for prep instructions)

1 (14-ounce) can full-fat coconut milk

1½ teaspoons fish sauce

¼ to ½ teaspoon cayenne pepper (depending on how spicy you like your stew)

01 In a large non-reactive bowl, combine ½ teaspoon of the lemon zest, ½ teaspoon of the lime zest, the lemon and lime juices, and 2 tablespoons of the chopped cilantro. Add the fish and shrimp and refrigerate, covered, for 30 minutes.

02 Melt the coconut oil in a large, heavy-bottomed pot over medium heat. Add the onion and sauté for 10 minutes, or until translucent and softened but not browned. Add the garlic and sauté for 30 seconds more.

03 Add the tomatoes, coconut milk, fish sauce, and cayenne pepper and simmer, covered, for 10 minutes.

04 Add the fish and shrimp, along with the marinade, to the pot. Bring to a simmer and cook for another 6 to 8 minutes, until the fish starts to flake and the shrimp are cooked through.

05 Serve the stew garnished with the remaining cilantro and citrus zest.

SAN FRANCISCO CIOPPINO

 YIELD: 4 to 6 servings | PREP TIME: 20 minutes | STOVETOP: 40 minutes

1 tablespoon avocado oil

1 large fennel bulb, thinly sliced, fronds reserved

4 large shallots, sliced (about 2 cups)

1 teaspoon salt

1½ cups dry white wine

3 cups Chicken Broth (page 40)

1 (28-ounce) can diced tomatoes or 2 pounds fresh tomatoes (see page 21 for prep instructions)

1 teaspoon red pepper flakes

2 pounds mussels, cleaned

1½ pounds shrimp, peeled and deveined

1½ pounds firm, mild white fish fillets, such as cod, snapper, or halibut, cut into ½- to ¾-inch pieces

¼ cup fresh lemon juice

2 tablespoons minced fresh parsley

01 Heat the oil in a large, heavy-bottomed pot over medium heat. When the oil is shimmering, add the fennel bulb, shallots, and salt and sauté until the shallots are translucent, 8 to 10 minutes.

02 Turn the heat up to high, add the wine, and cook for 1 minute, or until the alcohol smell lessens. Stir in the broth, tomatoes, and red pepper flakes. Bring to a simmer, then turn down the heat to medium-low and simmer, partially covered, for 20 to 25 minutes, stirring occasionally.

03 Add the mussels and continue to simmer until the shells open, 4 to 5 minutes.

04 Add the shrimp and fish and cook for an additional 4 to 5 minutes, until the shrimp and fish are cooked through. Discard any mussels that still haven't opened.

05 Turn off the heat and stir in the lemon juice and parsley. Chop the reserved fennel fronds. Serve the stew garnished with the fennel fronds.

GREAT WITH

Mini Boules

ORANGE AND OLIVE BEEF STEW

YIELD: 4 to 6 servings | PREP TIME: 10 minutes
STOVETOP: 2 hours 15 minutes | SLOW COOKER: 8 to 10 hours | PRESSURE COOKER: about 1 hour

2½ pounds beef stew meat

1 teaspoon salt

½ teaspoon ground black pepper

1 tablespoon avocado oil or tallow

1 large red onion, halved and thinly sliced

5 cloves garlic

1 tablespoon tomato paste

1 cup dry red wine

1 (14-ounce) can diced tomatoes or 1 pound fresh tomatoes (see page 21 for prep instructions)

1 large or 2 small blood oranges, sliced into thin half-moons (you can leave the peel on)

1 cup Castelvetrano olives, pitted

2 to 3 sprigs fresh thyme

01 Season the beef with the salt and pepper. Set aside.

02 Heat the oil in a large, heavy-bottomed pot over medium-high heat. Add the onion and cook for 5 minutes, or until it starts to brown and soften. Add the garlic and tomato paste and cook, stirring constantly, for another minute or two, until very fragrant.

03 Add the wine and cook until the liquid is reduced by half, which will take a few minutes.

04 Stir in the tomatoes and add the beef, orange slices, olives, and thyme sprigs. Turn the heat down to low and cook, partially covered, for 2 hours, or until the meat is very tender. Remove the orange slices and thyme sprigs before serving.

 Slow Cooker Instructions: *After completing Step 3, transfer the contents of the pot to a slow cooker. Add the tomatoes, beef, orange slices, olives, and thyme and cook on low for 8 to 10 hours, until the meat is very tender.*

 Pressure Cooker Instructions: *After completing Step 3, transfer the contents of the pot to a pressure cooker. Drain the tomatoes well and add them to the pressure cooker along with the beef, orange slices, olives, and thyme. Secure the lid and cook at high pressure for 30 minutes. Allow the pressure to naturally release before opening the lid. Switch to the sauté function and cook for 10 to 12 minutes, until the sauce reduces and thickens a bit.*

SPICY LAMB CURRY

YIELD: 4 to 6 servings | PREP TIME: 15 minutes
STOVETOP: about 1 hour | SLOW COOKER: 6 to 8 hours | PRESSURE COOKER: about 45 minutes

1 tablespoon coconut oil or ghee

1 medium onion, sliced

2 cloves garlic, minced

1 tablespoon grated fresh ginger

2 teaspoons ground coriander

1½ teaspoons turmeric powder

1 teaspoon ground cardamom

1 teaspoon ground cumin

½ teaspoon cayenne pepper

½ teaspoon ground cinnamon

⅛ teaspoon ground mace

Pinch of cloves

1 (14-ounce) can diced tomatoes or 1 pound fresh tomatoes (see page 21 for prep instructions)

1 cup Basic Beef Broth (page 42)

2 medium sweet potatoes, peeled and quartered

2 pounds boneless lamb stew meat

1 bunch spinach, stems discarded

Lower-Carb Modification:
Use pumpkin instead of sweet potatoes.

01 Melt the oil in a large, heavy-bottomed pot over medium-high heat. When the oil is shimmering, add the onion. Cook for 6 to 8 minutes, stirring occasionally, until golden brown and softened.

02 In a small bowl, combine the garlic, ginger, and spices. Add this mixture to the browned onions and cook for about 20 seconds, stirring constantly, until very fragrant.

03 Add the tomatoes and broth to the pot, scraping up any browned bits that are stuck to the bottom of the pot. Coarsely puree the mixture with an immersion blender.

04 Add the sweet potatoes and lamb. Partially cover the pot, reduce the heat to low, and cook for 45 minutes to 1 hour, until the lamb is tender. Stir in the spinach and cook until it's just wilted.

 Slow Cooker Instructions: *After completing Step 3, transfer the contents of the pot to a slow cooker. Add the sweet potatoes and lamb and cook on low for 6 to 8 hours, until the lamb is tender. Stir in the spinach and cook until it's just wilted.*

 Pressure Cooker Instructions: *Drain and discard the juice from the tomatoes and use just ½ cup of beef broth. After completing Step 3, transfer the contents of the pot to a pressure cooker. Add the sweet potatoes and lamb, secure the lid, and cook at high pressure for 25 minutes. Allow the pressure to release naturally for 10 minutes before opening the lid. Stir in the spinach and allow it to wilt.*

GREAT WITH

| 62 | 196 | 218 | 236 |

Dairy-Free Yogurt   *Cauliflower Rice*   *Raita*   *Naan*

PORK AND APPLE STEW
with cabbage and caraway

 YIELD: 4 to 6 servings | **PREP TIME:** 20 minutes | **STOVETOP:** about 35 minutes

¼ cup arrowroot starch

1 teaspoon salt, divided

¼ teaspoon paprika

¼ teaspoon mustard powder

2 pounds pork loin, cut into 1-inch pieces

3 tablespoons lard or avocado oil, divided

1 medium onion, diced

1 medium head cabbage (about 2 pounds), chopped

½ pound turnips (about 2 medium), peeled and diced

1 teaspoon caraway seeds, plus more for garnish

1 cup hard apple cider (see Tip)

1 tablespoon whole-grain mustard, plus more for serving

1 quart Chicken Broth (page 40)

2 apples, peeled and cut into sticks

¼ cup chopped fresh parsley

Chef's Tip: *If you prefer not to cook with alcohol, replace the hard apple cider with equal parts apple juice and water mixed with a tablespoon of apple cider vinegar.*

01 In a large bowl, whisk together the arrowroot starch, ½ teaspoon of the salt, paprika, and mustard powder. Toss the pork pieces with the starch mixture to coat.

02 Heat 1 tablespoon of the lard in a large, heavy-bottomed pot over medium-high heat. When the lard is shimmering, add half of the pork and sear until browned on all sides, about 5 minutes. Use a slotted spoon to remove the pork to a bowl. Add another tablespoon of the lard and sear the rest of the pork, removing it to the bowl when finished.

03 Add the remaining tablespoon of lard to the pot. Add the onion, cabbage, turnips, caraway seeds, and the remaining ½ teaspoon of salt. Sauté for 6 to 8 minutes, stirring occasionally, until the vegetables have softened a bit.

04 Pour in the cider and cook for 1 minute, or until the liquid reduces a bit.

05 Return the pork to the pot, along with any juices that have accumulated in the bowl.

06 Stir in the whole-grain mustard and add the broth. When the broth comes to a simmer, reduce the heat to medium-low. Cook, covered, for 10 minutes, or until the turnips are soft and the pork is cooked through.

07 Add the apples and cook, uncovered, for an additional 5 minutes, or until the apples are soft. Stir in the parsley and remove from the heat. Serve garnished with additional caraway seeds and additional mustard on the side, if desired.

ZENBELLY CHILI 2.0

YIELD: 4 to 6 servings | **PREP TIME:** 15 minutes
STOVETOP: about 2 hours | **SLOW COOKER:** 8 to 10 hours | **PRESSURE COOKER:** 50 minutes

One of the most loved recipes in *The Zenbelly Cookbook* is the chili, which is made with ground beef and has a similar flavor profile to this recipe. When re-creating it for this book, I decided to make it more in the style of chili Colorado, which is made with cubes of beef chuck instead of ground beef.

2 tablespoons lard, bacon fat, or avocado oil

1 large onion, diced

5 cloves garlic, roughly chopped

2 tablespoons tomato paste

2 tablespoons ancho chili powder

1 tablespoon ground coriander

1 tablespoon ground cumin

1½ teaspoons salt

1 teaspoon smoked paprika

⅛ teaspoon ground cinnamon

2½ pounds beef chuck, cut into 1-inch pieces

1 cup brewed coffee

1 (28-ounce) can diced tomatoes or 2 pounds fresh tomatoes (see page 21 for prep instructions)

2 tablespoons chipotle paste or chopped chipotle peppers in adobo sauce

FOR SERVING (OPTIONAL):

Dairy-Free Sour Cream (page 62)

Sliced green onions

Sliced avocado

01 Heat the lard in a large, heavy-bottomed pot over medium-high heat. Add the onion and cook for 5 minutes, or until it starts to soften. Add the garlic, tomato paste, chili powder, coriander, cumin, salt, smoked paprika, and cinnamon and cook for another minute or two, stirring constantly, until very fragrant.

02 Add the beef, coffee, tomatoes, and chipotle paste. Stir, scraping up any browned bits that are stuck to the bottom of the pan.

03 Bring the chili to a simmer. Turn the heat down to low and cook, partially covered, for 2 hours, or until the meat is very tender. Serve topped with sour cream, green onions, and avocado, if desired.

 Slow Cooker Instructions: *After completing Step 2, transfer the contents of the pot to a slow cooker. Cook on low for 8 to 10 hours, until the meat is very tender.*

 Pressure Cooker Instructions: *Use just ½ cup of coffee and drain the juices from the tomatoes. After completing Step 2, transfer the contents of the pot to a pressure cooker. Secure the lid and cook on high pressure for 35 minutes. Allow the pressure to release naturally for 10 minutes before opening the lid.*

Nut-Free Modification: *Omit the Dairy-Free Sour Cream.*

GREAT WITH

Drop Biscuits

Jalapeño Cheddar Biscuits

ROASTED TOMATILLO PORK CHILI VERDE

YIELD: 6 servings | **PREP TIME:** 20 minutes
STOVETOP: 1 hour 40 minutes | **SLOW COOKER:** 8 to 10 hours | **PRESSURE COOKER:** 55 minutes

1 pound tomatillos, papery husks removed, rinsed, and halved

1 medium onion, sliced into ½-inch-thick rings

2 poblano peppers (about ½ pound)

6 cloves garlic, unpeeled

2 jalapeño peppers, halved and seeded

1 handful fresh cilantro leaves, plus more for garnish

½ teaspoon dried oregano leaves

2 teaspoons salt, divided

1 cup Chicken Broth (page 40) or water

3 pounds pork shoulder, cut into 1-inch pieces

1 pound white or sweet potatoes, peeled and cut into bite-sized pieces

Lower-Carb Modification:
Use celery root instead of potatoes.

01 Preheat the broiler to high. Arrange the tomatillos, onion, poblano peppers, and garlic on a rimmed baking sheet. Broil for 5 to 7 minutes, until the veggies and garlic are charred. Flip the veggies and broil for another 5 minutes, or until the second side is charred.

02 Place the poblano peppers in a small bowl and cover with plastic wrap. This will build up enough steam to make the skins easy to rub off. When the garlic is cool enough to handle, pop the cloves out of the skins. Add the peeled garlic, onion, and jalapeño peppers to a blender. When the poblano peppers are cool enough to handle, rub off the skins and remove the stems and seeds. Add the poblano peppers to the blender with the rest of the vegetables, then add the cilantro, oregano, and 1 teaspoon of the salt. Pour in the broth and blend until smooth.

03 Season the pork with the remaining teaspoon of salt. Pour the tomatillo sauce into a large pot and add the pork and potatoes. Cover and cook at a bare simmer for about 90 minutes, until the pork and potatoes are tender. Serve garnished with cilantro.

Slow Cooker Instructions: *Complete Steps 1 and 2, but in Step 2 blend the tomatillo mixture with ½ cup chicken broth (instead of a full cup). Place the pork, potatoes, and tomatillo sauce in a slow cooker. Cook on low for 8 to 10 hours, until the pork and potatoes are tender.*

Pressure Cooker Instructions: *Complete Steps 1 and 2, but in Step 2 blend the tomatillo mixture with ½ cup chicken broth (instead of a full cup). Place the pork, potatoes, and tomatillo sauce in a pressure cooker. Secure the lid and cook at high pressure for 35 minutes. Allow the pressure to release naturally before opening the lid.*

GREAT WITH

62	214	232	234
Dairy-Free Sour Cream	*Spiced Pepitas*	*Flour Tortillas*	*Plantain Tortillas*

WHITE CHICKEN CHILI

YIELD: 4 to 6 servings | PREP TIME: 10 minutes | STOVETOP: about 1 hour 30 minutes | PRESSURE COOKER: about 1 hour

1 whole chicken (about 3 pounds)

2 teaspoons ancho chili powder, divided

1 teaspoon garlic powder

2 teaspoons salt, divided

1 small jicama, unpeeled

2 poblano peppers

1 tablespoon avocado oil

1 medium onion, cut into small dice

1 jalapeño pepper, minced

4 cloves garlic, minced

2 teaspoons ground coriander

2 teaspoons ground cumin

1 teaspoon smoked paprika

2 teaspoons cassava flour

1 quart Chicken Broth (page 40)

1 cup Cashew Cream (page 58)

¼ cup chopped fresh cilantro

FOR SERVING:

Diced avocado

Lime wedges

Sliced green onions

Nut-Free Modification: *Use coconut milk or flax milk (page 60) instead of cashew cream.*

GREAT WITH

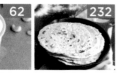

Dairy-Free Sour Cream — 62

Crispy Tortilla Chips — 232

01 Cook the chicken: Preheat the oven to 425°F. Season the chicken with 1 teaspoon of the chili powder, the garlic powder, and 1 teaspoon of the salt. Place the chicken and jicama (whole and unpeeled) in a baking dish and roast for 60 to 75 minutes, until the internal temperature of the chicken reaches 165°F. The jicama should be soft. When the jicama is cool enough to handle, peel it and cut it into small dice.

02 When the chicken is cool enough to handle, remove the meat from the bones, shred the meat, and discard the skin. Save the bones for making broth.

03 Make the sauce: Place the poblano peppers directly over a gas flame, turning occasionally, until blackened on all sides. Alternatively, if you don't have a gas stove, you can broil the peppers for about 5 minutes per side, until blackened. Transfer the peppers to a metal or glass bowl and cover with plastic wrap. When they're cool enough to handle, rub off the skins, remove the stem and seeds, and cut the peppers into small dice.

04 Heat the oil in a large, heavy-bottomed pot over medium-high heat. Add the onion and cook, stirring occasionally, for 8 to 10 minutes, until golden brown and softened.

05 Add the jicama, diced poblano peppers, jalapeño pepper, garlic, coriander, cumin, paprika, remaining teaspoon of chili powder, remaining teaspoon of salt, and cassava flour. Cook for another minute to toast the spices, then pour in the broth. Bring to a simmer and cover. Turn the heat down to medium-low and cook for 10 minutes, or until the jicama is very soft. (The cooking time will depend on how soft the jicama was after the initial roasting process.)

06 Once the jicama is soft, stir in the shredded chicken and cook the chili for another 2 to 3 minutes, until the chicken is heated through. Stir in the cashew cream and cilantro and cook for another 2 minutes.

07 Serve with diced avocado, lime wedges, and green onions.

Pressure Cooker Instructions: *To cook the chicken and jicama in an electric pressure cooker, peel the jicama and slice it in half. Place 1 cup of water in the insert of the pressure cooker, then set the rack in the pressure cooker. Season the chicken with 1 teaspoon of the chili powder, the garlic powder, and 1 teaspoon of the salt. Arrange the chicken and jicama on the rack of the pressure cooker. Secure the lid and cook on high pressure for 30 minutes. Allow the pressure to release naturally for 10 minutes before opening the lid. When the jicama is cool enough to handle, cut it into a small dice. Continue with Step 2.*

MOROCCAN VEGETABLE STEW

 YIELD: 4 to 6 servings | PREP TIME: 20 minutes | STOVETOP: about 30 minutes

2 tablespoons avocado oil

2 cups sliced carrots (½-inch rounds; about 3 large carrots)

2 cups diced red onions (about 1 medium)

4 cloves garlic, sliced

1 teaspoon salt

1 teaspoon ground cumin

1 teaspoon turmeric powder

½ teaspoon ground coriander

½ teaspoon paprika

⅛ teaspoon cayenne pepper

⅛ teaspoon ground cinnamon

Pinch of saffron

1 (28-ounce) can diced tomatoes or 2 pounds fresh tomatoes (see page 21 for prep instructions)

⅓ cup golden raisins

¼ cup currants

4 cups diced Japanese eggplant (about 1 large)

4 cups diced zucchini (about 4 medium)

3 cups diced sweet potato (about 1 large)

About 2 cups Roasted Vegetable Broth (page 36) or water

Chopped fresh mint, for garnish

Chopped toasted almonds, for garnish

01 Heat the oil in a large, heavy-bottomed pot over medium-high heat. Add the carrots and cook for 3 minutes, stirring occasionally. Add the onions and cook for 3 more minutes.

02 Add the garlic, salt, and spices and cook for 1 minute, or until very fragrant. Add the tomatoes, raisins, and currants and bring to a simmer.

03 Add the eggplant, zucchini, and sweet potato to the pot. Add enough broth to barely come up to the level of the veggies (about 2 cups). Cover and bring to a simmer.

04 Turn the heat down to low and simmer, covered, for 20 minutes or until all of the vegetables are tender, stirring two or three times during cooking. Serve garnished with fresh mint and toasted almonds.

Nut-Free Modification: *Omit the almonds.*

GREAT WITH

 62

 218 236

Dairy-Free Yogurt   Raita   Naan

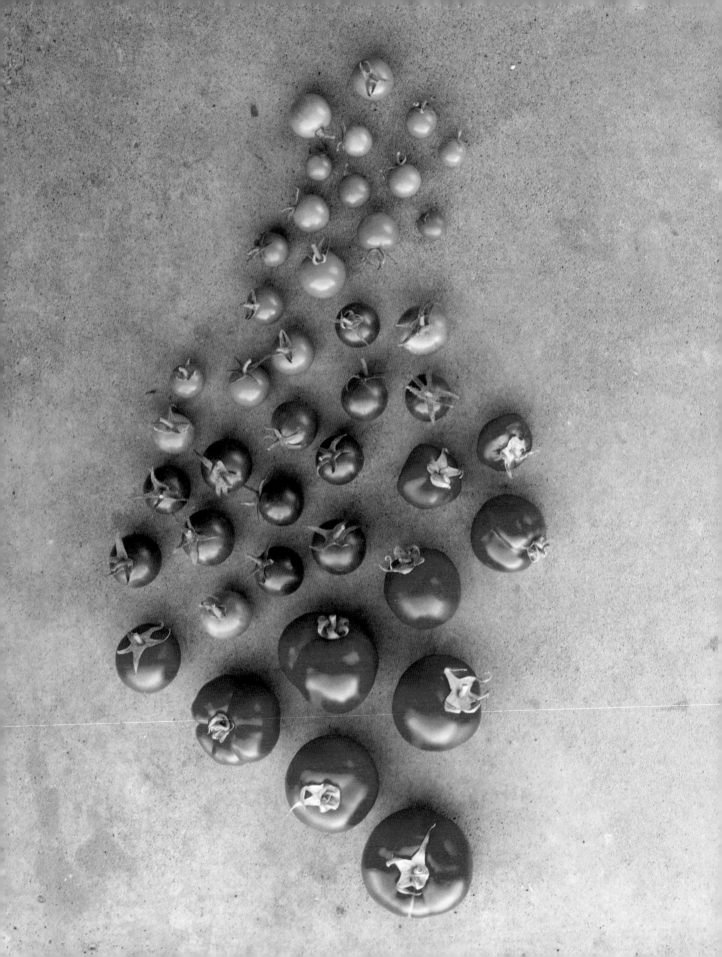

CHAPTER 5:

CHILLED SOUPS

There's a good possibility that the majority of the people who flip through this book will skip this chapter altogether. I get it—cold soup can feel like the opposite of what soup is supposed to be. To be honest, there are only a handful of days during the year that a bowl of chilled soup sounds good to me. But on those days, it sounds really, really good.

Those sweltering summer days when the humidity is 98 percent and walking outside feels similar to getting in a car that's been parked in the sun with its windows up—those are perfect chilled soup days. A bowl of ice-cold gazpacho in August, when the tomatoes are fresh off the vine and taste like something entirely different than what you get at the store in January—that is one of the best things in this world.

And if you're a salad-for-lunch person, cold soups are a great way to mix it up!

Many of the recipes in this chapter are regularly on my catering menus—even though lots of people don't think they like cold soup, almost everyone loves soup shooters, and a shot glass filled with Green Gazpacho (page 172) or Chilled Carrot-Cumin Soup (page 184) is always well received. Not only is cold soup a fun addition to a party menu, but it's also easy to make, and one batch of soup goes a long way when you're serving 2 ounces at a time. If you're stumped when planning your next dinner party menu, I recommend adding some cold soup to the menu, either in small cups or in shot glasses—they can all be made ahead, so they won't get in the way of your day-of prep.

GREEN GAZPACHO
with grapes and almonds

YIELD: 4 to 6 servings | PREP TIME: 15 minutes | CHILLING TIME: 2 hours

2 English cucumbers (about 1½ pounds), halved lengthwise and roughly chopped

1½ pounds green grapes, plus more for garnish

1 avocado, peeled, pitted, and quartered

1 small shallot, chopped (about ¼ cup)

2 cloves garlic

½ cup extra-virgin olive oil, plus more for drizzling

¼ cup white wine vinegar

1 teaspoon salt

Handful of mint leaves, roughly chopped, plus more for garnish

¼ cup salted roasted almonds, finely chopped, for garnish

01 Place all of the ingredients except the almonds in a blender and blend until smooth.

02 Refrigerate for at least 2 hours, until very cold.

03 Serve the chilled soup topped with sliced grapes, almonds, mint leaves, and a drizzle of olive oil.

AIP / Nut-Free Modification:
Omit the almonds.

GREEN CURRY AVOCADO SOUP

YIELD: 4 to 6 servings | PREP TIME: 10 minutes | CHILLING TIME: 1 hour

1 English cucumber (about 3/4 pound), peeled and chopped

1 avocado, peeled, pitted, and quartered

1 serrano chile, seeds and membrane removed, chopped

1 (14-ounce) can full-fat coconut milk

1½ cups cold water

3 tablespoons fresh lime juice

1 tablespoon green curry paste

2 teaspoons fish sauce

½ teaspoon salt

¼ cup fresh cilantro leaves, plus more for garnish

6 to 8 fresh Thai basil leaves, plus more for garnish

6 to 8 fresh mint leaves, plus more for garnish

01 Place all of the ingredients in a blender and puree until smooth.

02 Refrigerate for at least 1 hour, until very cold.

03 Serve the chilled soup garnished with cilantro, Thai basil, and mint leaves and/or herb ice cubes (see Tip).

Chef's Tip: *You can serve this soup garnished with herb ice cubes. To make the ice cubes, place an herb leaf or two in each reservoir of an ice cube tray, then fill the tray with water. Place the tray in the freezer until the cubes have frozen.*

GRILLED VEGETABLE GAZPACHO
with lemon, oregano, and olives

YIELD: 4 to 6 servings | PREP TIME: 15 minutes | GRILLING TIME: 10 to 20 minutes | CHILLING TIME: 2 hours

8 medium vine-ripened tomatoes (about 2½ pounds), sliced in half

2 zucchini (about ½ pound), cut into ½-inch rounds

2 yellow squash (about ½ pound), cut into ½-inch rounds

1 large Vidalia or yellow onion, cut into ½-inch slices

2 tablespoons avocado oil

2 bell peppers (red, yellow, orange, or a combination)

2 cloves garlic

¼ cup red wine vinegar

¼ cup fresh lemon juice

1 tablespoon packed fresh oregano leaves, divided

1 teaspoon salt

½ cup extra-virgin olive oil

¼ cup pitted Kalamata olives

1 teaspoon grated lemon zest

01 Preheat a grill to medium-high.

02 In a large bowl, toss the tomatoes, zucchini, yellow squash, and onion with the avocado oil.

03 Arrange the tomatoes, zucchini, yellow squash, and onion slices, along with the bell peppers, on the grill. Close the lid and cook for 5 minutes. Check the veggies and flip as needed. Continue cooking until they are moderately charred on all sides. As they finish cooking, remove them to a rimmed baking sheet. Depending on the heat level of your grill, it should take between 10 and 20 minutes for all of the veggies to cook.

04 Set aside a few slices of grilled onion.

05 Place the tomatoes and bell peppers in a heatproof bowl and cover with plastic wrap. When they are cool enough to handle, pull the skins off. Cut the peppers in half and remove the seeds. Place the tomatoes, peppers, remaining onion slices, garlic, vinegar, lemon juice, half of the oregano, and salt in a blender. Blend until smooth, slowly drizzling in the olive oil as the motor runs.

06 Cut the reserved onion slices, zucchini, yellow squash, and olives into small dice and place in a small bowl. Mince the remaining half of the oregano and add it, along with the lemon zest, to the diced vegetables and olives and mix everything together.

07 At this point, you can either combine the pureed and diced parts of the soup or keep them separate for presentation purposes, if you prefer. Refrigerate until very cold, at least 2 hours.

08 To serve: If you have chilled the pureed soup and the diced vegetable mixture separately, divide the diced vegetable mixture among four to six serving bowls and then pour in the soup.

Chef's Tip: *To keep the onion rings from falling through the grill grates, stick a toothpick through the slices before tossing them with the oil.*

WATERMELON GAZPACHO
with pistachios and basil

YIELD: 4 to 6 servings | PREP TIME: 15 minutes | CHILLING TIME: 2 hours

¼ cup minced Vidalia onions

¼ cup boiling water

3 tablespoons red wine vinegar

1 (3-pound) seedless watermelon

1 English cucumber (about ¾ pound), peeled

1 jalapeño pepper, seeded and quartered

¼ cup loosely packed fresh basil leaves, plus more for garnish if desired

3 tablespoons fresh lime juice

1 teaspoon salt

¼ teaspoon cayenne pepper

¼ cup extra-virgin olive oil

¼ cup shelled roasted and salted pistachios, minced

AIP Modification: *Omit the jalapeño pepper, cayenne pepper, and pistachios.*

Nut-Free Modification: *Omit the pistachios.*

01   In a small non-reactive bowl, combine the onions, boiling water, and vinegar. Set aside while you prep the remaining ingredients.

02   Roughly chop three-quarters of the watermelon, cucumber, and jalapeño pepper. Mince the remaining one-quarter of each. Mince half of the basil leaves, leaving the rest whole.

03   Place the chopped watermelon, chopped cucumber, chopped jalapeño pepper, whole basil leaves, lime juice, salt, and cayenne pepper in a blender. Blend until smooth, slowly drizzling in the olive oil while the motor runs.

04   In a non-reactive bowl, mix the blended ingredients with the minced watermelon, cucumber, jalapeño pepper, and minced basil. Stir in the onion mixture from Step 1. Refrigerate for 2 hours, or until very cold.

05   Serve sprinkled with the minced pistachios and additional basil.

CLASSIC GAZPACHO
with radishes and chives

YIELD: 4 to 6 servings | PREP TIME: 30 minutes | CHILLING TIME: 6 hours

1 medium red onion, minced

1/2 cup red wine vinegar

1/2 cup boiling water, plus more for soaking the tomatoes

12 medium tomatoes (about 3 pounds)

1 English cucumber (about 3/4 pound), peeled

1/2 cup extra-virgin olive oil

6 to 8 fresh basil leaves, roughly chopped

2 cloves garlic

1 teaspoon salt

1 yellow, orange or red bell pepper, seeded and minced

1 jalapeño pepper, seeded and minced

1/2 teaspoon Tabasco, plus more for serving

2 radishes, minced, for garnish

5 to 6 chives, minced, for garnish

01 In a large non-reactive bowl, combine the onion, vinegar, and 1/2 cup of boiling water. Set aside while you prep the vegetables.

02 Cut an X in the bottom of each tomato and place the tomatoes in a large bowl. Pour enough boiling water over them to cover and allow to sit for 2 to 3 minutes, until the skins start to loosen. Remove the tomatoes with tongs, place in a colander, and run cold water over them to cool them. Carefully remove and discard the skins and cut the tomatoes in half.

Alternatively, if it's not peak tomato season and your tomatoes aren't bursting with flavor, halve them and toss them with 1 tablespoon of extra-virgin olive oil. Place on a rimmed baking sheet and roast in a 425°F oven for 15 minutes. When the tomatoes are cool enough to handle, remove and discard the skins.

03 Roughly chop half of the cucumber and mince the other half.

04 Place the tomatoes, olive oil, chopped cucumber, basil, garlic, and salt in the bowl of a food processor. Pulse 10 to 12 times, until the mixture is a coarse puree.

05 Pour the tomato puree into the bowl with the onion mixture and add the bell pepper, jalapeño pepper, and minced cucumber. Stir in the Tabasco and cover. Refrigerate for at least 6 hours but preferably overnight to allow the flavors to marry.

06 When ready to serve, top each bowl with the minced radishes and chives. Serve with additional Tabasco.

SUMMER BORSCHT
with cucumber and dill

YIELD: 4 to 6 servings | PREP TIME: 15 minutes | STOVETOP: 30 to 40 minutes | CHILLING TIME: 2 hours

1 pound beets (about 6 medium), cleaned and tops removed

1 cup Chicken Broth (page 40)

3/4 cup unsweetened Dairy-Free Yogurt (page 62)

3 tablespoons fresh lemon juice (about 1 lemon)

1 tablespoon sherry vinegar

1 tablespoon honey

1/2 teaspoon salt

1 cup seeded and small-diced cucumber (about 1 large)

1/4 cup thinly sliced green onions (about 1 small bunch)

1 tablespoon minced fresh dill

01 Bring a large pot of salted water to a boil. Add the beets and cook until very soft, 30 to 40 minutes. Remove with a slotted spoon and set aside to cool. Reserve 1 cup of the cooking liquid. When the beets are cool enough to handle, rub off the skins using your hands or a paring knife.

02 Roughly chop one-quarter of the beets and cut the rest into small dice.

03 In a blender, combine the reserved cooking liquid, broth, roughly chopped beets, yogurt, lemon juice, sherry vinegar, honey, and salt. Blend until smooth.

04 Stir in the diced beets, cucumber, green onions, and dill, reserving a small amount of each for garnish, if desired. Refrigerate until very cold, at least 2 hours, before serving.

Chef's Tip: *For a quick, no-cook version of this soup, purchase vacuum-sealed steamed beets.*

AIP / Nut-Free Modification:
Use coconut milk instead of yogurt.

CHILLED CARROT-CUMIN SOUP
with carrot top–cilantro pesto

YIELD: 4 to 6 servings | PREP TIME: 10 minutes | STOVETOP: about 25 minutes | CHILLING TIME: 2 hours

1 tablespoon avocado oil

2 pounds carrots with tops, tops removed and reserved, carrots peeled or scrubbed and chopped

1 pound leeks (about 2 medium), white and light green parts only, cleaned and chopped (see Tip on page 38)

1 teaspoon cumin seeds

6 cups Veggie-Herb Broth (page 38) or equal parts Chicken Broth (page 40) and water

1 cup fresh orange juice

FOR THE PESTO:

Reserved carrot tops (from above)

1 cup packed fresh cilantro leaves (about 1 bunch)

¼ cup extra-virgin olive oil

¼ cup pine nuts

1 tablespoon fresh lime juice

¼ teaspoon salt

01 Make the soup: Heat the avocado oil in a large, heavy-bottomed pot over medium heat. When the oil is shimmering, add the carrots, leeks, and cumin seeds. Sauté, stirring occasionally, for 7 to 8 minutes, until the leeks have softened and the cumin seeds are fragrant.

02 Add the broth and orange juice and raise the heat to high. Bring to a boil, then turn down the heat so the soup is at a simmer. Cover and simmer for 15 to 20 minutes, until the carrots are very soft.

03 Puree the soup in batches in a blender until very smooth. Refrigerate until very cold, at least 2 hours.

04 Make the pesto: Remove and discard the tough stems of the carrot tops and clean the greens well. Measure out 1 cup of the cleaned, stemmed greens.

05 Put the cleaned carrot tops, cilantro, olive oil, pine nuts, lime juice, and salt in a food processor. Pulse 10 to 12 times, until you have a coarse puree.

06 Serve the chilled soup topped with the pesto.

Chef's Tip: *Freeze any remaining pesto if not using within 4 days. Prefer to use it up? It's also great on Minestrone with Orecchiette (page 114), Spring Chicken Soup with Lemon and Asparagus (page 94), or Moroccan Carrot Soup with Yogurt and Mace (page 70) or just stirred into some veggie noodles (page 194).*

AIP Modification: *Use ginger or turmeric instead of cumin, and use artichoke hearts instead of pine nuts in the pesto.*

Nut-Free Modification: *Use artichoke hearts instead of pine nuts in the pesto.*

SPICY PEACH GAZPACHO

YIELD: 4 to 6 servings | PREP TIME: 20 minutes | CHILLING TIME: 2 hours

6 ripe peaches (about 2 pounds), peeled and quartered (see Tip)

4 large yellow tomatoes (about 2 pounds), peeled, quartered, and seeds squeezed out (see Tip)

1 English cucumber (about 3/4 pound), peeled

1 large shallot, chopped

1 jalapeño pepper, seeded and chopped

2 tablespoons white wine vinegar

1 teaspoon salt

1/4 cup extra-virgin olive oil

1 yellow or orange bell pepper, seeded and cut into small dice

1 teaspoon cayenne pepper, or to taste (optional)

1 avocado, cut into small dice, for garnish

Coarse sea salt, for garnish

Lime wedges, for serving

01   In a blender, combine four of the peaches, two of the tomatoes, half of the cucumber, the shallot, and the jalapeño with the vinegar, salt, olive oil, and 1 cup of water. Puree until very smooth.

02   Cut the remaining peaches, tomatoes, and cucumber into small dice and place in a large glass bowl, along with the bell pepper. If desired, set aside a small amount of the diced mixture to garnish each bowl.

03   Combine the pureed mixture with the diced mixture and refrigerate for at least 2 hours.

04   When the gazpacho is chilled, taste and add the cayenne pepper, if needed (it will depend quite a bit on the spiciness of your jalapeño).

05   Garnish each bowl with diced avocado, coarse sea salt, and the reserved diced ingredients, if set aside previously. Serve with lime wedges.

Chef's Tip: *To peel the peaches and tomatoes, cut a shallow X in the bottom of each one and place them in a large bowl. Cover with boiling water and allow to sit for about 5 minutes. Remove with tongs. When they're cool enough to handle, peel off the skins.*

CHAPTER 6:

IN SOUP:
Noodles & Other Fun Additions

Adopting a grain-free lifestyle means that your days of slurping noodles in soup are over, right? Not necessarily! There are plenty of ways to get creative when it comes to fun additions to your bowl.

You'll find all sorts of fun stuff in this chapter—from simple and low-carb veggie noodles to incredibly flavorful wonton-inspired meatballs to homemade noodles that you won't believe are grain-free. These recipes range in difficulty from extremely simple, like the single-ingredient vegetable noodles, to moderately difficult, like the homemade noodles.

Many of the soup recipes in this book list recipes from this chapter as ingredients, meaning that they're important components of those specific recipes. (The matzo balls in Matzo Ball Soup are a good example of this.) But don't feel like you need to stop there—veggie noodles are great in countless soups, as are homemade grain-free flour–based noodles.

SERVING SUGGESTIONS: Some of the recipes in this chapter make more than enough for four to six servings of soup; you may have some extra after adding them to your bowls of soup. The reason for this? They all make excellent leftovers! Veggie noodles of all kinds (page 194) are great with some Pesto (page 206) stirred in. Wrapper-Less Wontons (page 200) make terrific snacks, and all you need to make Homemade Noodles (page 198) into a meal is your favorite pasta sauce.

MATZO BALLS

 YIELD: about 20 matzo balls | **PREP TIME:** 15 minutes | **COOK TIME:** 35 minutes

1 quart water or Chicken Broth (page 40)

1 pound Yukon Gold or Red Bliss potatoes (about 2 large), peeled and sliced

2 large eggs

½ cup potato starch

1 tablespoon extra-virgin olive oil

1 tablespoon minced fresh dill or ½ tablespoon dried dill weed

½ teaspoon salt

¼ teaspoon ground black pepper

¼ teaspoon onion powder

01 Place the water and potatoes in a large pot and bring to a boil. Cook for 20 minutes, or until the potatoes are tender. Turn off the heat, use a slotted spoon to remove the potatoes to a bowl, and allow them to cool for about 10 minutes. Reserve the cooking water—you'll use it to cook the matzo balls as well.

02 While the potatoes are cooling, whisk together the eggs, potato starch, olive oil, dill, salt, pepper, and onion powder. When the potatoes have cooled a bit, mash them into the egg mixture with a fork, making sure that everything is well incorporated.

03 Bring the pot of water back up to a simmer. To make the matzo balls, you can either roughly measure a heaping tablespoon of the dough and roll it into a ball with your hands or use a small (1-tablespoon) cookie scoop. You should end up with about 20 matzo balls.

04 Drop the matzo balls into the simmering water and cook for 15 minutes. Serve in piping-hot chicken soup.

ADD TO

Chicken Broth *Matzo Ball Soup*

WONTONS

YIELD: 2 dozen wontons (4 to 6 servings) | **PREP TIME:** 20 minutes (not including time to make the noodle dough)
COOK TIME: 3 minutes

FOR THE FILLING:

½ pound ground pork

½ cup minced green onions (2 to 3 large)

1 large egg yolk

1 tablespoon minced fresh ginger

1 tablespoon coconut aminos

1 teaspoon fish sauce

1 teaspoon unseasoned rice vinegar

1 teaspoon toasted sesame oil

Cassava flour, for dusting

1 batch Homemade Noodle dough (page 198)

01 Make the filling: Place all of the ingredients in a medium bowl and mix with your hands to combine.

02 Lightly dust your work surface with cassava flour. Roll out the noodle dough as thinly as possible into a rectangle that's roughly 15 by 10 inches. Use a sharp knife to cut the dough into 2½-inch squares. Cover with damp paper towels to keep the squares from drying out while you make the wontons.

03 Brush one of the squares with water to dampen it. Place about 1 teaspoon of filling just off center and fold over the other side to form a triangle. Press the edges together to seal. If desired, fold up the edges toward the filling and pinch off the extra dough. Repeat with the remaining squares and filling.

04 Bring a large pot of salted water to a boil. Gently add the wontons and cook for 3 minutes, or until the pasta and filling are fully cooked.

Chef's Tip: *This dough is fragile and can be difficult to work with, so don't rush, and don't be afraid to dampen the dough as you're working with it to make it more pliable.*

ADD TO

Chicken Broth

Pork Broth with Shiitake Mushrooms and Ginger

Dashi Broth

Shrimp Cilantro Broth

VEGGIE NOODLES

 YIELD: varies | **PREP TIME:** 5 minutes | **COOK TIME:** 5 to 45 minutes, depending on vegetable used

Going grain-free doesn't mean that you have to give up noodles! Lots of veggies make great noodle stand-ins and have the added benefit of contributing a serving of vegetables to your soup.

ZUCCHINI OR YELLOW SQUASH

(about ½ pound per serving): Cut the zucchini or yellow squash into noodles with a spiral slicer, vegetable peeler, or julienne peeler. Simmer the noodles in broth for 5 minutes or until soft.

SWEET POTATO

(about ¼ pound per serving): Peel the sweet potato and cut it into noodles with a spiral slicer or julienne peeler. Simmer the noodles in broth for 10 minutes or until soft.

SPAGHETTI SQUASH

(about ¼ pound per serving):
Preheat the oven to 400°F. Cut the spaghetti squash in half lengthwise, scoop out the seeds, and place the halves cut side down on a rimmed baking sheet. Add a small amount of water to the baking sheet and roast for 30 to 45 minutes, until the flesh of the squash is soft. Use a fork to remove the "noodles" from the peel.

CELERY ROOT

(about ¼ pound per serving):
Peel the celery root and cut it into noodles with a spiral slicer or julienne peeler. Simmer the noodles in broth for 10 minutes or until soft.

Chef's Tip: *You can add veggie noodles to any soup you'd like some noodles in! They are also great with Pesto (page 206).*

CAULIFLOWER RICE

 YIELD: 4 to 6 servings | **PREP TIME:** 5 minutes | **COOK TIME:** less than 5 minutes

1 medium head cauliflower

2 tablespoons avocado oil

½ teaspoon salt

01 Cut the head of cauliflower into quarters through the top and cut out the core.

02 Rice the cauliflower quarters one at a time by putting them through the chute of a food processor fitted with the shredder blade. Alternatively, grate the cauliflower using the large holes of a box grater.

03 Heat the avocado oil in a large skillet over medium-high heat. Add the cauliflower and salt and cook for 2 to 3 minutes, stirring often, until the cauliflower has softened a bit.

04 Add to soup right before serving, or serve on the side.

ADD TO

94 — Spring Chicken Soup with Lemon and Asparagus

114 — Minestrone with Orecchiette

118 — Meat and Potatoes Soup

SERVE WITH

154 — San Francisco Cioppino

158 — Spicy Lamb Curry

162 — Zenbelly Chili 2.0

164 — Roasted Tomatillo Pork Chili Verde

168 — Moroccan Vegetable Stew

HOMEMADE NOODLES OR ORECCHIETTE

 YIELD: ½ pound pasta (4 to 6 servings) | **PREP TIME:** 5 minutes, plus 20 minutes to rest | **COOK TIME:** 30 seconds

1 cup cassava flour

½ teaspoon salt

2 large whole eggs

1 large egg yolk

1 tablespoon extra-virgin olive oil

01 In a large bowl, whisk together the cassava flour and salt.

02 Make a well in the center of the flour mixture. Crack in the whole eggs and add the egg yolk and olive oil. Gently mix the eggs with a fork, then gradually turn the flour into them and mix gently to create a dough. If the dough is too wet, gradually add small amounts of cassava flour until the dough comes together. If it's too dry, gradually add small amounts of water until the dough is workable.

03 On a lightly floured surface, knead the dough until it is soft and pliable, about 2 minutes. Wrap in plastic wrap and set aside for 20 minutes.

TO MAKE NOODLES:

01 Roll out the dough as thinly as possible on a lightly floured surface (or you can use a pasta maker if you have one).

02 Using a sharp knife (or running it through the pasta maker, if using), slice the dough into noodles of ⅛- to ¼-inch width, depending on your preference.

03 Bring a pot of salted water to a boil and cook the noodles for 30 seconds. When ready to serve, add the cooked noodles to soup to heat through.

TO MAKE ORECCHIETTE:

01 Divide the dough into four equal portions. Roll out each portion into a log about ½ inch in diameter. Cut the logs into ¼-inch pieces.

02 Lightly flour the palm of one hand and the thumb of the opposite hand. Working one by one, press each piece of dough into your hand with your thumb to make an indentation. Repeat with the remaining portions of dough.

03 Bring a pot of salted water to a boil and cook the orecchiette for 30 seconds. When ready to serve, add the cooked orecchiette to soup to heat through.

ADD TO

Chicken Broth   Pho Broth   Minestrone   Tuscan Tomato Soup   Build Your Own Ramen

WRAPPER-LESS WONTONS

 YIELD: about 30 small meatballs (6 to 8 servings) | PREP TIME: 10 minutes | COOK TIME: 15 to 20 minutes

1 tablespoon avocado oil or coconut oil, melted

3 tablespoons coconut aminos

2 teaspoons toasted sesame oil

1 tablespoon fish sauce

1 tablespoon coconut flour

1 bunch green onions (about 10), minced

1½ tablespoons peeled and grated fresh ginger

1½ pounds ground pork

01 Preheat the oven to 425°F. Grease a rimmed baking sheet with the melted oil.

02 In a large bowl, mix together the coconut aminos, sesame oil, fish sauce, coconut flour, green onions, and ginger. Add the pork and mix with your hands until well combined.

03 Roll into golf ball–sized balls and place on the prepared baking sheet. Bake for 15 to 20 minutes, until thoroughly cooked and golden brown.

AIP Modification: *Omit the sesame oil.*

ADD TO

Chicken Broth | Pork Broth with Shiitake Mushrooms and Ginger | Dashi Broth | Shrimp Cilantro Broth | Classic Beef Pho | Egg Drop Soup

SWEET POTATO GNOCCHI

YIELD: 4 to 6 servings | PREP TIME: 20 minutes (not including time to soak cashews or cook sweet potato)
COOK TIME: less than 5 minutes

½ cup raw cashews, soaked in 1 cup water for at least 1 hour

1½ cups mashed or riced cooked sweet potato

1 large egg

½ cup cassava flour, plus more for dusting

01 Drain the cashews, place them in a food processor or blender with ¼ cup of water, and blend until very smooth.

02 Transfer the blended cashews to a medium bowl and add the sweet potato and egg. Gently whisk with a fork.

03 Slowly mix in the cassava flour until a soft dough forms.

04 Liberally dust your work surface with additional cassava flour and turn the dough onto it. Knead in more cassava flour as necessary so that you have a workable dough. Divide the dough into 4 equal portions.

05 Roll each portion of dough into a long log about 1 inch thick. Cut the logs into ½-inch pieces. Press each piece gently with a fork.

06 To cook the gnocchi, bring a medium pot of salted water to a boil. Cook the gnocchi in batches for about 1 minute each. Remove with a slotted spoon and refrigerate until ready to use. Use within 4 days, or freeze for up to 6 months.

Variation: Nut-Free Gnocchi. *Follow the method above, but omit the cashews, increase the amount of mashed or riced cooked sweet potato to 2 cups, and use ¾ to 1 cup cassava flour, starting with ¾ cup and adding up to ¼ cup more as needed to create a workable dough.*

Chef's Tip: *You can add these gnocchi to any of the broths; Roasted Vegetable Broth (page 36) and Chicken Broth (page 40) are a couple of my favorites.*

ADD TO

Harvest Chicken Soup

Chicken and Dumplings Soup (in place of the dumplings)

CHAPTER 7:

ON TOP:
Garnishes to Add a Perfect Pop of Flavor & Texture

Soup's done! Time to eat? Sure, dig in, but don't miss an opportunity to add a final pop of flavor—it can really be the pièce de résistance. For example, Tuscan Tomato Soup (page 124) is delicious on its own, but it's brought to a whole new level with a drizzle of Rosemary-Garlic Oil (page 208) at the end. The infused oil brings out the notes that are already in the soup and adds a layer of depth. Texture is another thing to think about. Hearty soups, stews, and chilis have different textures in the bowl, but they're almost always all cooked and tender. A sprinkle of Spiced Pepitas (page 214) on a bowl of Roasted Tomatillo Pork Chili Verde (page 164) or Chicken Tortilla Soup (page 134) adds a wonderful crunch that you wouldn't otherwise get.

The recipes in this chapter were written to be versatile. Some soups in the previous chapters include these as necessary garnishes, but most do not. Many of the toppings in this chapter are wonderful on a number of soups and stews in this book. For each one I've included recommendations for what they're great on, but don't be afraid to try new combinations! If you're enjoying a bowl of soup and have a lightbulb moment regarding the perfect garnish, go for it. You might find yourself adding some of the recipes in this chapter to your pantry staples.

PESTO

 YIELD: 1 cup | PREP TIME: 5 minutes

2 cups packed fresh basil leaves

¼ cup raw walnuts or pine nuts

1 or 2 cloves garlic, crushed

1 teaspoon salt

½ cup extra-virgin olive oil

01 Place the basil leaves, walnuts, garlic, and salt in the bowl of a food processor. Pulse 8 to 10 times, until it starts to form a paste. Slowly drizzle in the olive oil while the motor runs until everything is well incorporated.

02 Store the pesto in an airtight container in the refrigerator for up to 5 days.

AIP / Nut-Free Modification:
Use artichoke hearts instead of walnuts or pine nuts.

GREAT ON

Creamy Tomato Basil Soup

Super Green Soup

Spring Chicken Soup with Lemon and Asparagus

Minestrone with Orecchiette

ROSEMARY-GARLIC OIL

 YIELD: 3/4 cup | **PREP TIME:** 1 minute | **COOK TIME:** 45 minutes

3/4 cup extra-virgin olive oil

1 (4-inch) sprig fresh rosemary

5 cloves garlic, unpeeled

01 Place the ingredients in a small saucepan over low heat. Allow the oil to infuse for 45 minutes, or until the garlic is very soft.

02 Pour the mixture into a glass jar and refrigerate until ready to use. If you're not planning to use it within a week, strain out the garlic and rosemary before pouring the oil into the jar.

Chef's Tip: *Try this as a dip for any of the breads from the On the Side chapter.*

GREAT ON

 94

 114

 124

Spring Chicken Soup with Lemon and Asparagus

Minestrone with Orecchiette

Tuscan Tomato Soup

CURRY COCONUT CREAM

 YIELD: ½ cup | PREP TIME: 3 minutes | COOK TIME: 3 minutes

½ cup coconut cream (scooped from 1 [14-ounce] can chilled full-fat coconut milk)

1 teaspoon red curry paste

1 teaspoon fresh lime juice

01 In a small skillet over medium heat, whisk together the coconut cream and curry paste. Cook, whisking constantly, for 3 minutes. Stir in the lime juice and turn off the heat.

02 Chill and use within 4 days.

GREAT ON

88

Thai Pumpkin Soup

102

Tom Ka Gai

196

Cauliflower Rice

CROUTONS

 YIELD: about 2 cups | PREP TIME: 5 minutes | COOK TIME: 10 to 12 minutes

3 tablespoons melted ghee or avocado oil

1/2 teaspoon salt

1/4 teaspoon garlic powder

1/8 teaspoon ground black pepper

1 Baguette (page 246), cut into 1/2-inch chunks

01   In a large bowl, mix together the melted ghee, salt, garlic powder, and pepper. Add the chunks of bread and toss until well coated.

02   Heat a large skillet over medium heat. When the skillet is hot, add the croutons. Toast in the pan for 10 to 12 minutes, stirring often, until browned on all sides.

03   Serve immediately. If you wish to make the croutons in advance, store them in an airtight container for up to 5 days, or freeze for later. When you're ready to serve the croutons, place them on a rimmed baking sheet and pop them in a 350°F oven for 5 minutes to crisp them up.

GREAT ON

 68
 80
 82
 114
 124

Super Green Soup

Burnt Broccoli Soup with Lemon

30 Cloves of Garlic Soup

Minestrone with Orecchiette

Tuscan Tomato Soup

SPICED PEPITAS

 YIELD: about 1½ cups | **PREP TIME:** 5 minutes | **COOK TIME:** 5 to 7 minutes

1½ cups pumpkin seeds (pepitas)

1 tablespoon fresh orange, lemon, or lime juice

¾ teaspoon salt

½ teaspoon ground coriander

½ teaspoon ground cumin

¼ teaspoon smoked paprika

⅛ teaspoon chipotle chili powder

⅛ teaspoon ground cinnamon

1 teaspoon coconut sugar (omit if you're doing a sugar detox)

01 Preheat the oven to 375°F and line a rimmed baking sheet with parchment paper.

02 In a medium bowl, mix together the pumpkin seeds, orange juice, salt, spices, and coconut sugar (if using).

03 Spread the coated pumpkin seeds on the prepared baking sheet and bake for 5 to 7 minutes, until crisp and puffed. Allow to cool completely before storing in an airtight container in the pantry. If they lose their crunch after being stored, simply pop them in a 350°F oven for a few minutes to crisp them back up.

Chef's Tip: *These make great snacks, too!*

GREAT ON

Spicy Shrimp and Chorizo Soup   Zenbelly Chili 2.0   Roasted Tomatillo Pork Chili Verde   White Chicken Chili

FRIZZLED LEEKS

 YIELD: ³/₄ cup | **PREP TIME:** 5 minutes | **COOK TIME:** less than 5 minutes

l large leek, white and light green parts only

2 cups light olive oil or avocado oil, for frying

Salt (optional)

01 Clean the leek by slicing it in half lengthwise and running it under water as you separate the layers and wash out all of the dirt. Shake off the excess water, then cut the leek halves into 2-inch sections. Slice each section lengthwise as thinly as possible.

02 Heat the oil in a medium saucepan to 300°F. In two batches, fry the leeks for 1 to 1¹/₂ minutes per batch, until browned. Use a slotted spoon to remove the leeks to a plate lined with a paper towel.

03 Sprinkle the leeks with salt, if desired. They are best eaten within a few hours of being made.

GREAT ON

Asparagus Bisque with Cayenne and Lime | *30 Cloves of Garlic Soup* | *Potato Leek Soup* | *San Francisco Cioppino*

RAITA

 YIELD: about 1¼ cups | PREP TIME: 5 minutes | CHILLING TIME: 1 hour

¾ cup unsweetened Dairy-Free Yogurt (page 62) or coconut cream (scooped from 1 [14-ounce] can chilled full-fat coconut milk)

½ cup grated cucumber (¼ pound, or about 1 small), extra liquid squeezed out

¼ cup fresh mint, minced

2 tablespoons fresh lemon juice

¼ teaspoon salt

Pinch of ground black pepper

01　Combine all of the ingredients in a small mixing bowl.

02　Chill for at least 1 hour before serving and use within 2 days.

AIP Modification: *Use coconut cream instead of yogurt and omit the black pepper.*

Nut-Free Modification: *Use coconut cream instead of yogurt.*

GREAT ON

Spicy Lamb Curry　　*Moroccan Vegetable Stew*

SPICED YOGURT

 YIELD: 1 cup | PREP TIME: 3 minutes | CHILLING TIME: 1 hour

1 cup unsweetened Dairy-Free Yogurt (page 62) or coconut cream (scooped from 1 [14-ounce] can chilled full-fat coconut milk)

1 tablespoon fresh lemon juice

1 teaspoon grated lemon zest

½ teaspoon ground sumac

½ teaspoon paprika

¼ teaspoon salt

⅛ teaspoon cayenne pepper

01 Combine all of the ingredients in a small mixing bowl.

02 Chill for at least 1 hour before serving to allow the flavors to develop. Use within 4 days.

Nut-Free Modification: *Use coconut cream instead of yogurt.*

GREAT ON

Spicy Lamb Curry

Moroccan Vegetable Stew

CHAPTER 8:

ON THE SIDE:
Breads, Crackers & Dippers

When people adopt a Paleo or grain-free diet, soups and stews are a relatively effortless category of food that often doesn't require much adapting. So that part's easy. And quite often, a big bowl of soup is all you need; nothing seems to be missing.

Still, there is something utterly satisfying about a crusty piece of bread alongside a bowl of soup—something to sop up what's left in the bowl: garlic naan alongside a spicy curry, biscuits to dunk in your chili, or even a bread bowl in which to serve your clam chowder. Sure, every soup in this book is complete on its own, and the accompaniments in this chapter certainly aren't required if you don't miss breads in your life. But if you do, by all means enjoy a hunk of grain-free baguette with your favorite soup!

The recipes in this chapter use a variety of flours and ingredients that might not be in your pantry if you haven't been doing any Paleo baking. In an effort to appeal to a range of dietary restrictions, some breads and crackers are nut flour–based and therefore lower-carb, while others are nut-free and therefore heavier on the starch. It's important to note that none of the recipes in this chapter is intended to replace your regular meals; these recipes are meant as a lovely addition to an already nutritionally dense bowl of soup.

A NOTE ABOUT PSYLLIUM HUSKS: After many hours of recipe testing, I've found that nut-free and grain-free baked goods benefit greatly from the addition of a small amount of psyllium husk. This ingredient is simply insoluble fiber and replicates an elasticity and softness in baked goods that nothing else (that I have found) does. Psyllium husk is an ingredient that some people consider to be "not Paleo," and I don't necessarily disagree. However, I don't consider it to be that big an offender when used in this capacity, as a dough conditioner and not a dietary supplement. As with any ingredient, it is best to determine how it affects your own body before deciding whether it's a good choice for you.

BREADSTICKS

YIELD: 10 breadsticks | PREP TIME: 15 minutes, plus 75 to 90 minutes to rise | COOK TIME: 12 to 15 minutes

¼ cup warm water (110°F)

1 tablespoon honey

2 teaspoons active dry yeast

1 cup (165 g) blanched almond flour

½ cup (60 g) arrowroot starch, plus more for dusting

1 tablespoon ground psyllium husks

¾ teaspoon salt

1 tablespoon extra-virgin olive oil

1 large egg

1 tablespoon melted ghee or extra-virgin olive oil, for brushing

Chef's Tips: *After you set the yeast mixture aside to bloom in Step 1, it should get foamy and bubbly. If it doesn't, you'll need to start over; it means that your yeast is a dud or the water was too hot.*

You can sprinkle the breadsticks with coarse sea salt to add some nice texture and flavor. Use just ½ teaspoon of the salt in the dough and sprinkle coarse sea salt on top of the breadsticks after brushing them with olive oil or melted ghee and just before baking them. You need just enough coarse sea salt to get a crystal or two per bite.

01   In the bowl of a stand mixer (or a large bowl if you're using a hand mixer), use a whisk to combine the warm water, honey, and yeast. Set aside for 5 to 10 minutes, until the mixture is foamy.

02   In a medium bowl, use a whisk to combine the almond flour, arrowroot starch, psyllium husks, and salt.

03   When the yeast mixture is foamy, mix in the olive oil and egg, then add the dry ingredients to the bowl and mix on medium-high speed for 30 seconds, scraping down the sides of the bowl once to make sure that all of the ingredients are incorporated.

04   Scrape down the sides of the bowl with a spatula and gather as much of the dough into a ball as possible. It will be much wetter than a conventional bread dough.

05   Cover the bowl with a tea towel and set it in a warm, draft-free place. Allow the dough to rise for 75 to 90 minutes, checking it after 75 minutes to see if it's risen. It won't rise as dramatically as a conventional dough would, but it will have changed, becoming more aerated and a bit larger.

06   Preheat the oven to 425°F. Line a baking sheet with lightly oiled parchment paper.

07   Divide the dough into ten sections. Liberally dust your hands with arrowroot starch, then roll each section of dough into a long skinny stick. The breadsticks will rise when cooked, so make them skinnier than you want the end result to be.

08   Transfer the breadsticks to the prepared baking sheet and brush them with the olive oil or melted ghee.

09   Bake for 12 to 15 minutes, until the breadsticks are golden brown. If not eating right away, store in an airtight container at room temperature for up to 1 day, or refrigerate for up to 4 days. These breadsticks freeze well and can be reheated in a 350°F oven for a few minutes.

SEEDED CRACKERS

 YIELD: about 50 crackers | PREP TIME: 10 minutes | COOK TIME: about 15 minutes

1 tablespoon extra-virgin olive oil

1 large egg

3/4 cup blanched almond flour

1/2 cup arrowroot starch

1/4 cup sesame, caraway, black caraway, or poppy seeds, or a combination

1/4 teaspoon onion flakes

1/2 teaspoon salt

01 Preheat the oven to 350°F.

02 In a large mixing bowl, whisk together the olive oil and egg.

03 Add the almond flour, arrowroot starch, seeds, onion flakes, and salt and mix until the dough comes together. Knead the dough once or twice to make sure that the ingredients are well incorporated.

04 Roll out the dough between two sheets of parchment paper to a thickness of 1/8 inch. Make the dough as rectangular as possible.

05 Discard the top sheet of parchment and use a sharp knife to cut the dough into 1-inch squares. (Make sure to cut all the way through, but do not pull them apart yet.)

06 Slide the bottom sheet of parchment onto a baking sheet. Bake for 8 to 10 minutes, until the crackers begin to brown.

07 Turn the oven temperature down to 325°F and bake for an additional 6 to 8 minutes, until the crackers are crisp and light golden brown.

08 Remove from the oven and allow to cool on the baking sheet before breaking the crackers apart. Store in an airtight container for up to 1 week.

GARLIC AND CHIVE CRACKERS

 YIELD: about 50 crackers | PREP TIME: 10 minutes | COOK TIME: about 15 minutes

1 large egg

1 tablespoon extra-virgin olive oil

3/4 cup blanched almond flour

1/2 cup arrowroot starch

1 tablespoon minced fresh chives

3/4 teaspoon garlic powder

1/2 teaspoon salt

01 Preheat the oven to 350°F.

02 In a large mixing bowl, beat the egg with the olive oil.

03 Stir in the remaining ingredients and mix until the dough comes together. Knead it once or twice to make sure that the ingredients are well incorporated.

04 Roll out the dough between two sheets of parchment paper to a thickness of about $1/8$ inch. Try to get it as close to a rectangle as possible. Discard the top sheet of parchment.

05 Use a sharp knife to cut the dough into 1-inch squares. (Make sure to cut all the way through, but do not pull them apart yet.)

06 Slide the bottom sheet of parchment onto a baking sheet and bake for 8 to 10 minutes, until the crackers begin to brown.

07 Turn the heat down to 325°F and bake for an additional 6 to 8 minutes, until the crackers are crisp and light golden brown.

08 Remove from the oven and allow to cool on the baking sheet before breaking the crackers apart. Store in an airtight container for up to 1 week.

OYSTER CRACKERS

YIELD: 1 cup crackers | PREP TIME: 15 minutes, plus 30 minutes to chill | COOK TIME: about 30 minutes

¼ cup plus 1 tablespoon cassava flour

¼ cup arrowroot starch

1 teaspoon coconut sugar

¼ teaspoon salt

¼ teaspoon cream of tartar

teaspoon baking soda

1 tablespoon cold ghee

1 teaspoon apple cider vinegar

3 to 4 tablespoons ice water, as needed

01 Preheat the oven to 375°F.

02 In the bowl of a food processor, pulse the cassava flour, arrowroot starch, coconut sugar, salt, cream of tartar, and baking soda to combine.

03 Add the ghee and apple cider vinegar and pulse a few more times, until the mixture resembles crumbs.

04 Slowly drizzle in the water 1 tablespoon at a time. The consistency of the dough should be such that you can squeeze it together without it cracking. Once you've added enough water to get it to that point, shape the dough into a disc and wrap it in plastic wrap. Refrigerate for 30 minutes.

05 Unwrap the dough and roll it out between two sheets of parchment paper into a rectangle that is ¼ inch thick. Remove the top sheet of parchment and cut the crackers into ½-inch squares or diamonds. Discard the top sheet of parchment and transfer the bottom sheet to a baking sheet. Separate the crackers, spreading them out on the parchment paper. This step can be a bit time-consuming since the dough is on the soft side. The best way to do it is to scoop up a row with a small offset spatula and gently push them off the tip of the spatula, leaving a bit of space between the crackers.

06 Bake for 10 to 12 minutes, until the crackers are just starting to brown. Turn off the heat and prop open the oven door a bit with a wooden spoon. Allow the crackers to cool in the oven for about 20 minutes—they will continue to crisp even though the heat is off.

07 Store the crackers in an airtight container for up to 1 week.

Chef's Tip: *If you store your ghee at room temperature, put a tablespoon in a small dish and place it in the freezer 30 minutes or so before you start making the crackers.*

FLOUR TORTILLAS

 YIELD: 4 tortillas | PREP TIME: 5 minutes | COOK TIME: about 10 minutes

½ cup cassava flour

1 tablespoon avocado oil

1 teaspoon fresh lime juice

¼ teaspoon salt

01   Place all of the ingredients in a medium bowl. Add ¼ cup of water and mix well to combine. Knead the dough a few times with your hands, adding more water or cassava flour if necessary to create a smooth, workable dough.

02   Roll the dough into a log and divide it into four equal portions. Roll out each portion between two sheets of parchment paper, making it as thin as possible.

03   Heat a large (preferably cast-iron) skillet over high heat. Cook each tortilla for 1 to 2 minutes per side, until it puffs up and browns in spots.

Variation: Crispy Tortilla Chips or Strips. *Preheat the oven to 400°F. Brush the cooked tortillas lightly with oil and sprinkle with salt, garlic powder, and chili powder, if desired. Cut each tortilla into 6 triangles or into thin strips, if preferred (the latter is a great option if using for Chicken Tortilla Soup, page 134). Spread the triangles or strips on a baking sheet and bake for 4 minutes, then flip and bake for another 2 to 3 minutes, until the chips are golden brown and crispy. If your tortillas are on the thicker side, they may take longer to crisp up; just check them every minute or so until they are nice and crispy.*

PLANTAIN TORTILLAS

 YIELD: 12 to 16 small tortillas | PREP TIME: 15 minutes | COOK TIME: about 20 minutes

3 to 4 barely ripened yellow plantains (2 to 2½ pounds)

⅓ cup egg whites (2 to 3 large eggs)

3 tablespoons lard or fat of your choice, melted but not hot, plus more for greasing the parchment paper

1 teaspoon fresh lime juice

½ teaspoon salt

01 Preheat the oven to 350°F.

02 Peel the plantains by cutting off the tops and bottoms and slicing through the skin along the length of the plantain. Roughly chop the plantains and place in the bowl of a food processor or high-speed blender.

03 Add the egg whites, melted lard, lime juice, and salt. Blend until very smooth.

04 Line two baking sheets with parchment paper (or work in batches if you only have one baking sheet). Grease the parchment paper liberally.

05 Using a medium (2-ounce) ladle or cookie scoop, drop four ¼-cup portions of batter onto each pan, leaving plenty of room between them. Using the ladle and/or a rubber spatula, smooth out the batter into thin circles. Get them as thin as you can while keeping them intact.

06 Bake for 10 to 12 minutes, or until they are dry to the touch and just starting to brown at the edges. If using two pans at once, switch their positions halfway through.

07 Repeat with the remaining batter, making sure to grease the parchment paper each time.

Chef's Tips: *These tortillas store, freeze, and reheat beautifully. Reheat them over a gas flame for 20 seconds on each side, turning as needed, or in the oven or on a grill.*

Although you may have to adjust the cooking time, you can make these tortillas any size you like.

NAAN

 YIELD: 4 pieces | PREP TIME: 5 minutes | COOK TIME: about 15 minutes

¼ cup unsweetened Dairy-Free Yogurt (page 62)

1 large egg white

1 teaspoon maple syrup

1 cup blanched almond flour

3/4 cup arrowroot starch

½ teaspoon salt

¼ teaspoon baking soda

1 teaspoon ghee or avocado oil

01 In a medium bowl, whisk together the yogurt, egg white, and maple syrup.

02 In a separate bowl, whisk together the almond flour, arrowroot starch, salt, and baking soda. Add to the wet ingredients and stir to combine.

03 Divide the dough into four equal portions and use your hands to flatten each portion to a thickness of about ½ inch.

04 Heat the ghee in a large (preferably cast-iron) skillet over medium-high heat. Cook the naan for 1½ to 2 minutes per side, until it puffs up and browns in spots. Serve warm.

Variation: Garlic Naan. *Prepare the naan as described above. Heat 2 teaspoons of ghee over medium heat, then add 3 to 4 cloves of minced garlic. Cook for 1 to 2 minutes, until the garlic is fragrant and just beginning to brown. Stir in 1 tablespoon of minced chives. Brush the garlic mixture onto the warm naan.*

DROP BISCUITS

 YIELD: 6 biscuits | PREP TIME: 10 minutes | COOK TIME: 12 to 15 minutes

2½ cups blanched almond flour

¾ cup arrowroot starch

½ teaspoon baking soda

½ teaspoon salt

¼ cup (½ stick) cold unsalted butter, ghee, duck fat, or lard (see Tip)

2 large eggs

2 tablespoons honey

01 Preheat the oven to 350°F and line a baking sheet with parchment paper.

02 In a large bowl, whisk together the almond flour, arrowroot starch, baking soda, and salt.

03 Use a box grater to grate the cold butter into the dry ingredients. With your hands, gently mix the butter into the flour mixture, making sure not to overwork it. It should resemble coarse crumbs, no larger than peas.

04 In a small bowl, beat the eggs and honey.

05 Gently mix the egg mixture into the dry ingredients, but do not overmix. You want the dough just to come together.

06 Using a large spoon or an ice cream scoop with a lever, drop the dough onto the prepared baking sheet in 6 equal portions. It helps to dampen your hands and shape the biscuits a bit. Bake for 12 to 15 minutes, until the biscuits are golden brown and cooked through. They are best eaten right away but can be stored in an airtight container in the refrigerator for up to 3 days. Reheat in the oven for a few minutes before serving.

Chef's Tip: *If you use ghee, duck fat, or lard for this recipe, pop it in the freezer for 10 minutes to get it very cold.*

JALAPEÑO CHEDDAR BISCUITS

YIELD: 6 large biscuits | **PREP TIME:** 10 minutes | **COOK TIME:** 12 to 15 minutes

2½ cups blanched almond flour

¾ cup arrowroot starch

½ teaspoon baking soda

½ teaspoon salt

¼ cup (½ stick) cold unsalted butter, ghee, duck fat, or lard (see Tip)

3 large eggs

2 tablespoons honey

3 ounces mild or medium-sharp cheddar cheese, shredded (about ½ packed cup)

2 jalapeño peppers, seeded and minced

01 Preheat the oven to 350°F and line a baking sheet with parchment paper.

02 In a large bowl, whisk together the almond flour, arrowroot starch, baking soda, and salt.

03 Use a box grater to grate the cold butter into the dry ingredients. With your hands, gently mix the butter into the flour mixture, making sure not to overwork it. It should resemble coarse crumbs, no larger than peas.

04 In a small bowl, whisk together the eggs and honey.

05 Gently mix the egg mixture, cheese, and jalapeño peppers into the dry ingredients, but do not overmix. You want the dough just to come together.

06 Using a large spoon or an ice cream scoop with a lever, drop the dough onto the prepared baking sheet in 6 equal portions. It helps to dampen your hands and shape the biscuits a bit. Bake for 12 to 15 minutes, or until the biscuits are golden brown and cooked through. They are best eaten right away but can be stored in an airtight container in the refrigerator for up to 3 days. Reheat in the oven for a few minutes before serving.

Chef's Tip: *If you use ghee, duck fat, or lard for this recipe, pop it in the freezer for 10 minutes to get it very cold.*

PULL-APART DINNER ROLLS

 YIELD: 9 small rolls | PREP TIME: 15 minutes | COOK TIME: 18 to 22 minutes

½ cup warm water (110°F)

2 tablespoons honey

1 tablespoon active dry yeast

2 large whole eggs

1 large egg white

6 tablespoons melted (but not hot) ghee or palm shortening

1 teaspoon apple cider vinegar

⅔ cup (90 g) cassava flour

½ cup (75 g) potato starch, plus more for dusting

2 tablespoons ground psyllium husks

1 teaspoon salt

Make-Ahead Instructions:
If you'd like to prepare these rolls the day before, complete Steps 1 through 6 and refrigerate the unbaked rolls overnight. Allow to come to room temperature for about an hour before baking as directed in Step 7.

01 Preheat the oven to 375°F and grease an 8-inch square glass or ceramic baking dish with ghee.

02 In the bowl of a stand mixer (or a large bowl if you're using a hand mixer), use a whisk to combine the warm water, honey, and yeast. Set aside for 5 to 10 minutes, until the mixture is foamy.

03 In a medium bowl, beat the whole eggs and egg white with the melted ghee and vinegar.

04 In another medium bowl, combine the cassava flour, potato starch, ground psyllium husks, and salt.

05 When the yeast mixture is foamy, add the egg mixture and flour mixture to the bowl with the yeast mixture. Mix on low speed to incorporate the ingredients. Scrape down the sides of the bowl, then turn the mixer to high speed and beat for 4 to 5 minutes, until the mixture comes together as a very sticky dough.

06 Dust your work surface with potato starch and turn the dough onto it. Roll the dough into a log and divide it into nine equal portions. Dust your hands with potato starch, roll each dough portion into a ball, and place it in the prepared baking dish.

07 Bake the rolls for 18 to 22 minutes, until golden brown on top and cooked through. Allow to cool in the pan before pulling apart. These rolls are best fresh out of the oven.

Variation: Seeded Rolls. *To turn these pull-apart dinner rolls into seeded rolls, reserve the egg yolk when you separate it from the egg white. Before baking the rolls, combine the yolk with 1 tablespoon of water, then brush the tops of the rolls with the egg wash. Sprinkle 2 teaspoons of poppy seeds, sesame seeds, or a combination of both on the rolls, then bake as directed above.*

Chef's Tip: *After you set the yeast mixture aside to bloom in Step 1, it should get foamy and bubbly. If it doesn't, you'll need to start over; it means that your yeast is a dud or the water was too hot.*

RYE BREAD

YIELD: One round loaf (4 to 6 servings) | PREP TIME: 20 minutes, plus 30 minutes to rise | COOK TIME: 25 minutes

½ cup warm water (110°F)

1 tablespoon honey

1 tablespoon active dry yeast

1 large whole egg

2 large egg whites (reserve 1 yolk for the egg wash)

¼ cup avocado oil

1 tablespoon apple cider vinegar

1 teaspoon molasses

⅔ cup (90 g) cassava flour

½ cup (75 g) potato starch, plus more for dusting

1 teaspoon salt

2 tablespoons psyllium husks, ground

2 tablespoons ground caraway seeds, plus more whole seeds for the top

01   In the bowl of a stand mixer (or a large bowl if you're using a hand mixer), use a whisk to combine the warm water, honey, and yeast. Set aside for 5 to 10 minutes, until the mixture is foamy.

02   In a medium bowl, whisk together the egg, egg whites, avocado oil, vinegar, and molasses.

03   In a small bowl, whisk together the cassava flour, potato starch, salt, ground psyllium husks, and ground caraway seeds.

04   Add the flour mixture and the egg mixture to the bowl of the stand mixer. Mix on low speed to incorporate the ingredients, scraping down the sides when necessary. Turn the mixer to high speed and mix for 4 to 5 minutes, or until the dough has thickened. It should be looser and stickier than a traditional bread dough, but significantly thicker than where it started.

05   Line a baking sheet with parchment paper. Liberally dust a clean surface with potato starch and turn the dough onto it. Sprinkle some potato starch on top of the dough and dust your hands. Gently knead the dough, adding more potato starch if it's still sticky. It will be softer than traditional bread dough. Form the dough into a ball and place on the prepared baking sheet. Cut an X into the top of the dough.

06   In a small bowl, whisk together the reserved egg yolk with a tablespoon of water. Brush the top of the dough with the egg wash and sprinkle with the whole caraway seeds.

07   Allow the dough to rise, uncovered, in a warm, draft-free place for 30 minutes. It will spread out quite a bit and become more aerated. Preheat the oven to 375°F after about 15 minutes.

08   Bake for 25 minutes, or until the loaf is golden brown and sounds hollow when you tap it with a wooden spoon. Allow to cool before serving.

Chef's Tip: *After you set the yeast mixture aside to bloom in Step 1, it should get foamy and bubbly. If it doesn't, you'll need to start over; it means that your yeast is a dud or the water was too hot.*

BAGUETTES

YIELD: 2 large baguettes | PREP TIME: 20 minutes, plus 30 minutes to rise | COOK TIME: 35 to 40 minutes

1 cup warm water (110°F)

2 tablespoons honey

2 tablespoons active dry yeast

6 large egg whites (about 1 cup)

⅓ cup plus 1 tablespoon extra-virgin olive oil

2 tablespoons apple cider vinegar

1¼ cups (165 g) cassava flour

1 cup (150 g) potato starch

¼ cup psyllium husks, ground (about 3 tablespoons after grinding)

2 teaspoons salt

SPECIAL EQUIPMENT:

Baguette pan

01   Line a double baguette pan with lightly greased parchment paper.

02   In the bowl of a stand mixer (or a large bowl if you're using a hand mixer), use a whisk to combine the warm water, honey, and yeast. Set aside for 5 to 10 minutes, until the mixture is foamy.

03   In a large bowl, whisk together the egg whites, olive oil, and vinegar. In a separate bowl, combine the cassava flour, potato starch, ground psyllium husks, and salt.

04   Add the egg white mixture and flour mixture to the bowl with the yeast mixture. Mix on low speed for 1 minute, or until the ingredients are well incorporated. Scrape down the sides of the bowl, then turn the mixer to high speed and beat for 2 minutes, or until you have a very sticky dough.

05   Dump half of the dough into each side of the baguette pan. With well-floured hands, spread the dough so that it almost fills the pan, leaving about 2 inches of space on each end. Use a sharp knife to cut three diagonal slashes into the top of each loaf.

06   Allow the dough to rise, uncovered, in a warm, draft-free place for 30 minutes, or until increased in size by about one-third. Preheat the oven to 350°F after 15 minutes.

07   Bake for 35 to 40 minutes, until the loaves are brown and sound hollow when tapped with a wooden spoon. Allow to cool completely before removing from the pan.

08   If not eating right away, store in a plastic bag for up to 3 days, or freeze for later use. Reheat in a 350°F oven, placed directly on the oven rack, for a few minutes.

Chef's Tip: *After you set the yeast mixture aside to bloom in Step 1, it should get foamy and bubbly. If it doesn't, you'll need to start over; it means that your yeast is a dud or the water was too hot.*

MINI BOULES OR BREAD BOWLS

YIELD: 2 mini boules (4 servings) or 2 bread bowls | PREP TIME: 20 minutes, plus 30 minutes to rise
COOK TIME: 20 to 24 minutes

½ cup warm water (110°F)

1 tablespoon honey

1 tablespoon active dry yeast

2 large eggs

¼ cup avocado oil

2 tablespoons apple cider vinegar

⅔ cup (90 g) cassava flour

½ cup (75 g) potato starch, plus more for dusting

1 tablespoon plus 1 teaspoon finely ground psyllium husks

1 teaspoon salt

01   In the bowl of a stand mixer (or a large bowl if you're using a hand mixer), use a whisk to combine the warm water, honey, and yeast. Set aside for 5 to 10 minutes, until the mixture is foamy.

02   In a medium bowl, whisk together the eggs, avocado oil, and vinegar.

03   In a small bowl, whisk together the cassava flour, potato starch, psyllium husks, and salt.

04   Add the flour mixture and the egg mixture to the bowl with the yeast. Mix on low to incorporate the ingredients, scraping down the sides of the bowl when necessary. Turn the mixer to high speed and mix for 4 to 5 minutes, until the dough has thickened. It should be looser and stickier than a traditional bread dough, but significantly thicker than where it started.

05   Line a baking sheet with parchment paper. Liberally dust a clean work surface with potato starch and turn the dough onto it. Dust your hands with potato starch, then form the dough into a log. Divide the dough in half. Knead each one and shape into a ball. Place on the prepared baking sheet and cut an X into the top of each loaf.

06   Allow the dough to rise, uncovered, in a warm, draft-free place for 30 minutes. Preheat the oven to 375°F after 15 minutes.

07   Bake for 20 to 24 minutes, until the loaves are golden brown. Allow to cool before serving. If filling with soup, cut off the top and scoop out the center, leaving a 1-inch thickness on the sides and bottom.

Chef's Tips: *After you set the yeast mixture aside to bloom in Step 1, it should get foamy and bubbly. If it doesn't, you'll need to start over; it means that your yeast is a dud or the water was too hot.*

If making bread bowls, save the center of the bread for breadcrumbs; pulse in a food processor until coarsely ground and freeze until ready to use.

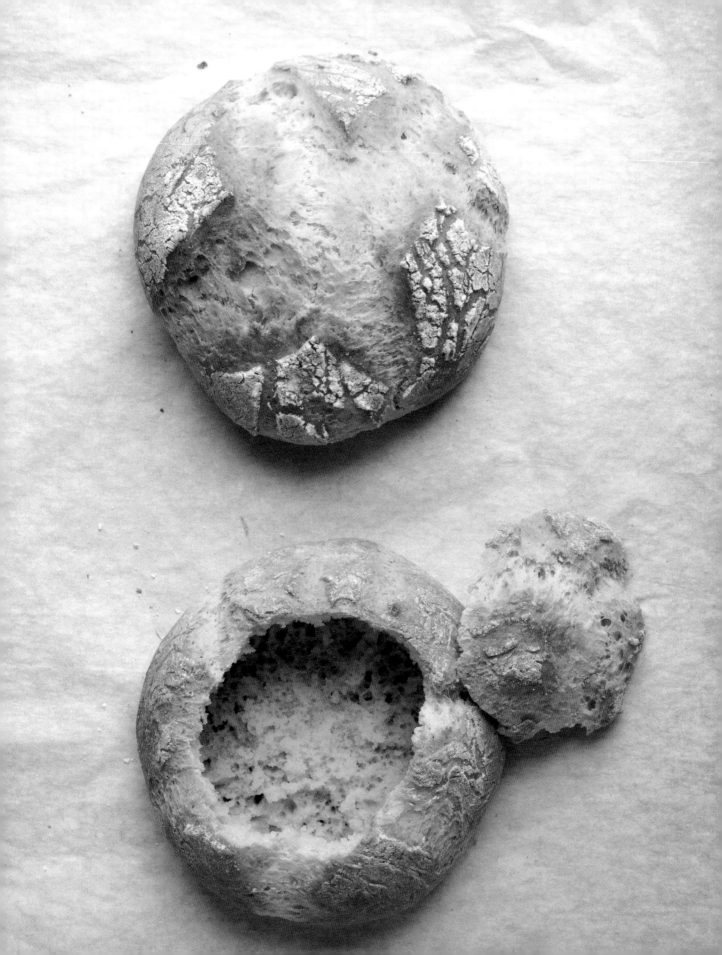

SPICY ROASTED OKRA

 YIELD: 4 to 6 servings | PREP TIME: 5 minutes | COOK TIME: about 15 minutes

½ pound fresh okra, sliced in half lengthwise

1 teaspoon paprika

¼ teaspoon granulated garlic

¼ teaspoon salt

⅛ teaspoon dried oregano leaves

⅛ teaspoon cayenne pepper (optional)

2 tablespoons avocado oil

01   Preheat the oven to 425°F and line a rimmed baking sheet with parchment paper.

02   In a large bowl, toss the okra with the seasonings and oil. Spread it cut side down on the lined baking sheet. Place the baking sheet in the bottom third of the oven and roast the okra for 8 minutes, then flip it over and roast for another 6 minutes, until it is golden brown and crisp.

GREAT WITH

Super Green Soup — Smoky Shrimp and Chorizo Soup — Oxtail and Smoked Pork Gumbo — Moroccan Vegetable Stew

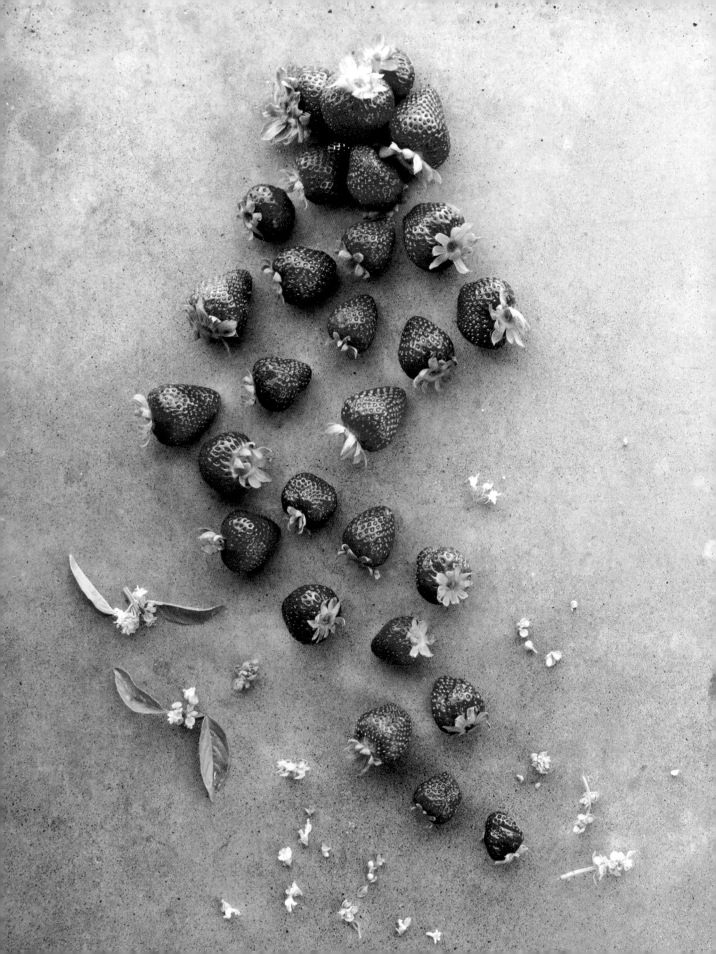

CHAPTER 9:

SWEET SOUPS AND COOKIES

Sure, this is a book about soup, but that doesn't mean you have to skip dessert! Serving a sweet soup as the dessert course is a fun way to keep things fresh and interesting at a dinner party. And, for the sake of texture, each soup in this chapter is paired with a cookie that complements it perfectly.

The soup and cookie combinations were created to be enjoyed together, but of course you can use your creativity and mix and match if you'd like. Short on time? Skip the cookies and serve a bowl of good chocolates with your sweet soup instead.

The classic example of a sweet soup is often cold and fruit based, but the Chocolate Soup on page 262 is warmed, perfect for a cold night.

A NOTE ON SERVING SIZES: All of the recipes in this chapter serve four to six people, just like the recipes in the other chapters. However, since you wouldn't eat a big bowl of sweet soup as you would a savory soup or stew, the actual yield is smaller.

CRUSHED STRAWBERRY SOUP
with rose shortbread cookies

YIELD: 4 to 6 servings | PREP TIME: 10 minutes | CHILLING TIME: 2 hours

2 pounds fresh strawberries, hulled and quartered

1 cup fresh orange juice

1/4 cup fresh lemon juice

2 tablespoons honey

1 to 2 tablespoons fruity red wine (optional)

Splash of sparkling white wine or rosé (optional)

Fresh mint leaves, for garnish (optional)

01 Place the strawberries, orange juice, lemon juice, honey, and red (but not sparkling) wine, if using, in a food processor. Pulse 10 to 12 times, until the mixture has a uniform but still somewhat coarse texture.

02 Refrigerate until very cold, at least 2 hours. If adding sparkling wine, add it to the soup just before serving. Garnish each bowl with mint leaves, if desired.

AIP Modification: *Omit the wine and sparkling wine.*

ROSE SHORTBREAD COOKIES

 YIELD: 4 to 6 servings | PREP TIME: 10 minutes | COOK TIME: 12 to 14 minutes

1 1/2 cups blanched almond flour

1/2 cup arrowroot starch, plus more for dusting

1/4 cup coconut sugar

1/8 teaspoon salt

1/2 teaspoon rose water

1/4 cup (1/2 stick) cold unsalted butter or palm shortening

1 large egg

Chef's Tip: *Rose water can be found online or at Middle Eastern markets.*

01 Preheat the oven to 350°F and line a baking sheet with parchment paper.

02 In a medium bowl, whisk together the flour, arrowroot starch, sugar, and salt. Add the rose water and whisk again.

03 Use a box grater to grate the cold butter into the flour mixture. Use your hands to incorporate the butter until the mixture resembles coarse crumbs.

04 Add the egg and mix with a fork until it comes together into a workable dough. Lightly knead the dough to achieve a uniform consistency, but do not overwork it.

05 Liberally dust a clean work surface with arrowroot starch. Shape the dough into a relatively flat disc and dust it lightly with more starch. Roll out the dough to a thickness of 1/8 inch. Use a small cookie cutter or thin-rimmed glass to cut the dough into small cookies. The shape is up to you.

06 Transfer the cookies to the prepared baking sheet and bake for 12 to 14 minutes, until they are golden brown on the bottom. Allow to cool completely on the baking sheet.

07 Store any uneaten cookies in an airtight container at room temperature for up to 5 days.

ORANGE PISTACHIO SOUP
with raw cacao truffles

YIELD: 4 to 6 servings | PREP TIME: 10 minutes, plus 1 hour to soak pistachios | CHILLING TIME: 1 hour

¼ cup shelled roasted and salted pistachios, plus minced pistachios for garnish

1 cup boiling water

1 tablespoon maple syrup

⅛ teaspoon salt

1 ruby red grapefruit

1 large Cara Cara or Valencia orange

1 blood orange or other small orange

AIP / Nut-Free Modification:
Use 1 cup of full-fat coconut milk in place of the pistachios and water.

01 Place the pistachios in a medium bowl and pour the boiling water over them. Set aside to soak for 1 hour.

02 Drain the pistachios and place them in a blender with 1 cup of cool water, the maple syrup, and the salt. Blend on high speed for 1 minute, until smooth. Strain through a fine-mesh strainer and discard any pulp.

03 Supreme the citrus: Using a sharp knife, cut off the top and bottom of each grapefruit and orange. Working from the top down and following the shape of the fruit, cut off strips of peel, making sure to remove the pith as well. Working over a bowl, cut between the membranes to release the segments. Squeeze the remaining juice from the peels and membranes into the bowl.

04 Combine the citrus segments and their juices with the pistachio milk and chill for at least 1 hour before serving.

05 Serve in shallow bowls with minced pistachios sprinkled on top.

RAW CACAO TRUFFLES

 YIELD: 1 dozen small truffles | PREP TIME: 5 minutes

1 cup raw cacao powder, plus more for coating

¼ cup maple syrup

1 tablespoon coconut oil

1 tablespoon unsalted nut butter or sunflower seed butter

Pinch of fine sea salt

Nut-Free Modification: *Use sunflower seed butter instead of nut butter.*

01 In a food processor fitted with the S blade, process all of the ingredients. The mixture should look similar to damp dirt.

02 With the motor running, add 1 teaspoon of water at a time until the mixture comes together into a solid mass.

03 Roll the mixture into 12 small balls, then roll the balls in cacao powder, dusting off any excess so they're just barely coated.

04 Store in an airtight container in the refrigerator. Remove the truffles from the fridge 1 hour before serving.

SUMMER BERRY SOUP
with chewy ginger cookies

YIELD: 4 to 6 servings | PREP TIME: 5 minutes | CHILLING TIME: 1 hour

8 ounces strawberries, hulled

8 ounces blueberries (about 1½ cups), divided

6 ounces raspberries (about 2½ cups), divided

6 ounces blackberries (about 1½ cups), divided

1 cup white grape juice

1 teaspoon balsamic vinegar

¼ teaspoon vanilla extract

Fresh mint leaves, for garnish (optional)

01 Place the strawberries, three-quarters of the blueberries, three-quarters of the raspberries, three-quarters of the blackberries, and the white grape juice in a blender. Blend until smooth.

02 Strain the puree through a fine-mesh strainer and discard the seeds. Stir the balsamic vinegar and vanilla extract into the soup.

03 Chill for at least 1 hour, until very cold.

04 When ready to serve, thin the soup with more white grape juice or cold water, if needed—it might have thickened while chilling. Pour into small bowls and garnish with the remaining berries. Garnish with mint leaves, if desired.

CHEWY GINGER COOKIES

 YIELD: 1 dozen cookies | PREP TIME: 5 minutes | COOK TIME: 8 to 10 minutes

¼ cup softened ghee

¼ cup coconut sugar

2 tablespoons maple syrup

1½ teaspoons molasses

1 large egg yolk

1 cup blanched almond flour

¼ cup arrowroot starch

1¼ teaspoons ginger powder

¼ teaspoon ground cloves

⅛ teaspoon salt

01 Preheat the oven to 375°F and line a baking sheet with parchment paper.

02 In the bowl of a stand mixer (or a large bowl if you're using a hand mixer), beat the ghee and coconut sugar for 2 to 3 minutes, until smooth and lighter in color.

03 Add the maple syrup, molasses, and egg yolk and beat until well combined and fluffy, about 1 minute.

04 In a medium bowl, whisk together the almond flour, arrowroot starch, ginger powder, cloves, and salt. Add the dry ingredients to the wet ingredients and stir to combine.

05 Drop tablespoon-sized spoonfuls of the dough onto the baking sheet and flatten each cookie to a thickness of about ¼ inch.

06 Bake for 8 to 10 minutes, until the cookies are just starting to brown around the edges. (Rotate the pan 180 degrees halfway through baking if your oven doesn't heat evenly.) Allow the cookies to cool on the baking sheet before serving.

ROASTED PLUM SOUP
with cinnamon roll cookies

YIELD: 4 to 6 servings | PREP TIME: 10 minutes | COOK TIME: 8 to 10 minutes | CHILLING TIME: 1 hour

1½ pounds plums (about 9 large), divided

1 tablespoon honey mixed with 1 tablespoon hot water

½ cup cold water

½ cup white grape juice

¼ cup fresh lemon juice

½ teaspoon vanilla extract

½ teaspoon ginger powder

01 Preheat the oven to 450°F and line a rimmed baking sheet with parchment paper.

02 Slice 1 pound (about 6) of the plums in half lengthwise and remove the stones. In a medium bowl, toss the plum halves with the honey mixture.

03 Arrange the plums on the prepared baking sheet. Reserve the liquid in the bowl. Roast the plums for 8 to 10 minutes, until very soft. Allow the plums to cool.

04 While the roasted plums are cooling, cut the remaining plums into small dice and set aside.

05 When the roasted plums are cool enough to handle, pull off and discard the skins. Transfer the plums and any liquid on the baking sheet to the bowl with the remaining honey mixture.

06 In a blender, puree the roasted plums with the water, white grape juice, lemon juice, vanilla extract, and ginger powder.

07 In a large bowl, mix together the pureed plum mixture and the diced plums. Chill for at least 1 hour, until very cold.

CINNAMON ROLL COOKIES

YIELD: about 2 dozen small cookies | PREP TIME: 15 minutes, plus 1 hour to chill | COOK TIME: 10 to 12 minutes

2 tablespoons melted coconut oil

2 tablespoons honey

1 large egg

1 cup blanched almond flour

1 cup arrowroot starch

2 tablespoons coconut flour

⅛ teaspoon salt

2 tablespoons softened ghee or coconut oil

1 tablespoon coconut sugar

1 tablespoon ground cinnamon

01 In a large bowl, whisk together the oil, honey, and egg.

02 In another bowl, whisk together the almond flour, arrowroot starch, coconut flour, and salt, then add to the wet ingredients and mix with a wooden spoon until a dough forms. Shape the dough into a disc and wrap in plastic wrap. Refrigerate for 30 minutes.

03 While the dough is chilling, mix together the ghee, coconut sugar, and cinnamon in a small bowl.

04 Roll out the chilled dough between two sheets of parchment paper into a rectangle about 10 by 8 inches. Spread the cinnamon mixture evenly over the dough, leaving about ½ inch bare at the top.

05 Starting with the edge opposite the ½-inch gap, roll up the dough lengthwise as tightly as possible. Wrap in plastic wrap and freeze until very firm, about 30 minutes.

06 Line a rimmed baking sheet with parchment paper and preheat the oven to 350°F.

07 Take the dough out of the freezer and remove the plastic wrap. Use a sharp knife to cut the dough into ¼-inch slices. Arrange the slices on the prepared baking sheet. (The cookies will not spread while baking.)

08 Bake for 10 to 12 minutes, until golden brown. Allow to cool on the baking sheet before serving.

CHOCOLATE SOUP
with graham cracker marshmallow dippers

 YIELD: 4 to 6 servings | **PREP TIME:** 5 minutes | **COOK TIME:** less than 5 minutes

8 ounces dark chocolate, chopped

½ cup unsweetened cocoa powder

½ cup coconut sugar

3 tablespoons tapioca starch

1 teaspoon vanilla extract

⅛ teaspoon salt

4 (14-ounce) cans full-fat coconut milk

01 In a medium bowl, whisk together all of the ingredients except for the coconut milk.

02 In a medium pot, heat the coconut milk until steaming. Whisk in the chocolate mixture and heat for 1 to 2 minutes, until thickened.

GRAHAM CRACKER MARSHMALLOW DIPPERS

YIELD: 32 dippers | PREP TIME: 15 minutes, plus 2 hours to set | COOK TIME: 18 to 20 minutes

01 Preheat the oven to 350°F and line an 8-inch square baking dish with parchment paper, leaving some paper hanging over the sides of the pan.

02 In a medium bowl, whisk together the melted coconut oil and maple syrup.

03 In a separate bowl, whisk together the almond flour, arrowroot starch, coconut sugar, cinnamon, and salt. Add to the wet ingredients and use your hands to incorporate them. The dough will be a bit crumbly.

04 Firmly press the dough into the prepared baking dish and bake for 18 to 20 minutes, until golden brown. Set aside to cool while you prepare the marshmallow layer.

05 Pour ¼ cup of water into the bowl of a stand mixer (or a large bowl if you're using a hand mixer), then sprinkle it with the gelatin. Set aside.

06 In a small saucepan, heat ¼ cup of water, the maple syrup, and the salt until it reaches 235°F.

07 Using the whisk attachment with your mixer on a low setting, start to slowly beat the gelatin mixture to break it up. With the machine running, slowly pour in the hot maple syrup mixture, letting it run down the side of the bowl. When the gelatin is completely dissolved, turn the mixer to high. Beat the mixture until it has tripled in size and is white, about 5 minutes.

08 Pour the marshmallow mixture over the graham cracker base, smooth it out with a spatula, and allow it to rest at room temperature for at least 2 hours.

09 When the marshmallow layer is set, use the parchment paper to lift the graham cracker base out of the pan and use a very sharp knife to cut into 1 by 2-inch rectangles. For optimal texture, serve the bars within 1 day.

FOR THE GRAHAM CRACKER BASE:

3 tablespoons coconut oil, melted

1 tablespoon maple syrup

1 cup blanched almond flour

¼ cup arrowroot starch

2 tablespoons coconut sugar

1 teaspoon ground cinnamon

⅛ teaspoon salt

FOR THE MARSHMALLOW LAYER:

1½ tablespoons gelatin

3/4 cup maple syrup

⅛ teaspoon salt

RESOURCES

SHOPPING GUIDE

Almond flour (blanched, finely ground)
Anthony's Goods
anthonysgoods.com

Animal fats (duck fat, lard, tallow)
Epic
epicbar.com

Arrowroot starch
Bob's Red Mill
bobsredmill.com

Avocado oil
Primal Kitchen
primalkitchen.com

Bone broth
Osso Good Bones
ossogoodbones.com

Canned tomatoes and tomato paste (BPA-free)
Bionaturae
bionaturae.com

Costco
costco.com

Trader Joe's
traderjoes.com

Cassava flour
Otto's Naturals
ottosnaturals.com

Coconut aminos
Coconut Secret
coconutsecret.com

Coconut milk
Native Forest
edwardandsons.com or *amazon.com*

Extra-virgin olive oil
Kasandrinos
kasandrinos.com

Fish sauce
Red Boat
redboatfishsauce.com

Gelatin
Vital Proteins
vitalproteins.com

Great Lakes
greatlakesgelatin.com

Ghee
Tin Star Foods
tinstarfoods.com

Potato starch
Bob's Red Mill
bobsredmill.com

Psyllium husks
Indus organics
indusorganics.com

Tapioca starch
Bob's Red Mill
bobsredmill.com

SEASONAL SOUPS

Spring

Asparagus Bisque
with Cayenne and Lime
72

Super Green Soup
68

Green Curry Avocado Soup
174

Grilled Vegetable Gazpacho
with Lemon, Oregano, and Olives
176

Spring Chicken Soup
with Lemon and Asparagus
94

Vietnamese Crab and Asparagus Soup
128

Moroccan Vegetable Stew
168

Crushed Strawberry Soup
254

Summer

180

Classic Gazpacho
with Radishes and Chives

186

Spicy Peach Gazpacho

178

Watermelon Gazpacho
with Pistachios and Basil

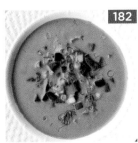
182

Summer Borscht
with Cucumber and Dill

172

Green Gazpacho
with Grapes and Almonds

134

Chicken Tortilla Soup

184

Chilled Carrot-Cumin Soup
with Carrot Top–Cilantro Pesto

258

Summer Berry Soup

Fall

88

Thai Pumpkin
Soup

86

Mushroom
Bisque

78

Roasted Cauliflower Soup
with Lime and Pine Nuts

138

Beef Borscht

70

Moroccan Carrot Soup
with Yogurt and Mace

96

Harvest Chicken Soup
with Sweet Potato Gnocchi

74

Creamy Tomato
Basil Soup

160

Pork and Apple Stew
with Cabbage and Caraway

260

Roasted Plum
Soup

Winter

Sweet Potato Soup
with Chipotle and Lime

Burnt Broccoli Soup
with Lemon

French Squash Soup
with Pears and Herbes de Provence

30 Cloves of Garlic Soup

Potato Leek Soup
with Frizzled Leeks

Sweet and Sour Cabbage Soup

Orange and Olive Beef Stew

Meat and Potatoes Soup

Caldo Verde
(Portuguese Potato Soup)

Orange Pistachio Soup

Chocolate Soup

SPECIAL DIETS

*An **X** means that the recipe is compliant as written; an **M** means that it is compliant when the modifications noted on the recipe page are made.*

	Page	AIP	Lower-Carb	Egg-Free	Nut-Free
Roasted Vegetable Broth	36	M	X	X	X
Veggie-Herb Broth	38	X	X	X	X
Chicken Broth	40	M	X	X	X
Basic Beef Broth	42	M	X	X	X
Roasted Beef and Mushroom Broth	44	M	X	X	X
Pork Broth with Shiitake Mushrooms and Ginger	46	M	X	X	X
Dashi Broth	48	X	X	X	X
Wild Mushroom Broth	50	M	X	X	X
Fish Broth	52	M	X	X	X
Shrimp Cilantro Broth	54	M	X	X	X
Pho Broth	56		X	X	X
Cashew Cream	58		X	X	
Flax Milk	60		X	X	X
Dairy-Free Yogurt and Sour Cream	62		X	X	
French Squash Soup with Pears and Herbes de Provence	66	M		X	X
Super Green Soup	68	M	X	X	X
Moroccan Carrot Soup with Yogurt and Mace	70	M		X	
Asparagus Bisque with Cayenne and Lime	72	M	X	X	X
Creamy Tomato Basil Soup	74		X	X	X
Tomato and Roasted Pepper Soup	76		X	X	X
Roasted Cauliflower Soup with Lime and Pine Nuts	78	M	X	X	M
Burnt Broccoli Soup with Lemon	80	X	X	X	X
30 Cloves of Garlic Soup	82	M	X	X	X
Potato Leek Soup with Frizzled Leeks	84			X	M
Mushroom Bisque	86	M	X	X	M
Thai Pumpkin Soup	88	M		X	X
Sweet Potato Soup with Chipotle and Lime	90			X	X
Spring Chicken Soup with Lemon and Asparagus	94	X	X	X	X
Harvest Chicken Soup with Sweet Potato Gnocchi	96	M	M	M	M
Sweet and Sour Cabbage Soup	98		M	X	X
Tom Yum (Thai Hot and Sour Soup)	100	M	X	X	X
Tom Ka Gai (Thai Chicken Coconut Soup)	102	M	M	X	X
Classic Beef Pho	104		M	X	X

	Page	AIP	Lower-Carb	Egg-Free	Nut-Free
New England Clam Chowder	106	M	M	X	X
Manhattan Clam Chowder	108		M	X	X
Italian Wedding Soup	110		X		
French Onion Soup	112	M	M	M	X
Minestrone with Orecchiette	114		M	M	X
Spicy Shrimp and Chorizo Soup	116		X	X	X
Meat and Potatoes Soup	118		M	X	X
Caldo Verde (Portuguese Potato Soup)	120			X	X
Hot and Sour Soup	122		X	M	X
Tuscan Tomato Soup	124		X	X	X
Matzo Ball Soup	126				X
Vietnamese Crab and Asparagus Soup	128	M	X	M	X
Egg Drop Soup	130		X		X
Build Your Own Ramen	132	M	M	M	X
Chicken Tortilla Soup	134		M	X	X
Chicken and Dumplings Soup	136			X	
Beef Borscht	138			X	M
Burmese Chicken Noodle Soup	140	M	M	M	X
Lobster Bisque	142		X	X	X
Oxtail and Smoked Pork Gumbo with Spicy Roasted Okra	144		X	X	X
West African Cashew Soup	146		X	X	
Five-Spice Beef Stew with Sweet Potatoes and Baby Bok Choy	150			X	X
Brazilian Fish Stew	152		X	X	X
San Francisco Cioppino	154		X	X	X
Orange and Olive Beef Stew	156		X	X	X
Spicy Lamb Curry	158		M	X	X
Pork and Apple Stew with Cabbage and Caraway	160			X	X
Zenbelly Chili 2.0	162		X	X	M
Roasted Tomatillo Pork Chili Verde	164		M	X	X
White Chicken Chili	166		X	X	M
Moroccan Vegetable Stew	168			X	M
Green Gazpacho with Grapes and Almonds	172	M		X	M
Green Curry Avocado Soup	174		X	X	X
Grilled Vegetable Gazpacho with Lemon, Oregano, and Olives	176		X	X	X
Watermelon Gazpacho with Pistachios and Basil	178	M		X	M
Classic Gazpacho with Radishes and Chives	180		X	X	X
Summer Borscht with Cucumber and Dill	182	M		X	M
Chilled Carrot-Cumin Soup with Carrot Top-Cilantro Pesto	184	M		X	M
Spicy Peach Gazpacho	186			X	X

ACKNOWLEDGMENTS

To Simon: You're my rock, babe, and I couldn't do what I do without you. (Sorry about the mess.)

To Elijah: It's a wonderful feeling to know that I can call you to ask any question, food related or not, and you will know the answer. I don't know how you find the time to answer my phone calls, but I'm so grateful that you do.

To the restaurant owners who trusted me with the daily soup: Deb and Rex, and Samantha: I'm so grateful for all that you taught me about consistency, creativity, and integrity.

To my blogger family/community: I'm truly blown away at how supportive a group of people can be. Every question I have or favor I need is just an IM away from being answered or delivered, and that is a very sweet feeling.

To Jen Robins: For continuing to be my work wife, even though we're not still writing a book together. I love that I can always count on you to be there to bounce ideas off of, ask dumb questions, and send terrible selfies to.

To the staff at Victory Belt: Every author should be lucky enough to work with the Victory Belt team. My sincere thanks to the entire staff who had a hand in putting this book together. And especially to Erich and Pam for being there to answer every phone call and email about every teensy detail.

To my readers: You all are the reason I keep writing books, and your support is everything. I am the worst blogger ever and don't deserve your loyalty, but am grateful for it nonetheless. (More recipes coming soon, I pinky promise.)

RECIPE THUMBNAIL INDEX

CHAPTER 1:
BROTHS AND BASICS

 36
Roasted Vegetable Broth

 38
Veggie-Herb Broth

 40
Chicken Broth

 42
Basic Beef Broth

 44
Roasted Beef and Mushroom Broth

 46
Pork Broth with Shiitake Mushrooms and Ginger

 48
Dashi Broth

 50
Wild Mushroom Broth

 52
Fish Broth

 54
Shrimp Cilantro Broth

 56
Pho Broth

 58
Cashew Cream

 60
Flax Milk

 62
Dairy-Free Yogurt and Sour Cream

CHAPTER 2:
BLENDED SOUPS

 66
French Squash Soup with Pears and Herbes de Provence

 68
Super Green Soup

 70
Moroccan Carrot Soup with Yogurt and Mace

 72
Asparagus Bisque with Cayenne and Lime

 74
Creamy Tomato Basil Soup

 76
Tomato and Roasted Pepper Soup

 78
Roasted Cauliflower Soup with Lime and Pine Nuts

 80
Burnt Broccoli Soup with Lemon

 82
30 Cloves of Garlic Soup

 84
Potato Leek Soup with Frizzled Leeks

 86
Mushroom Bisque

 88
Thai Pumpkin Soup

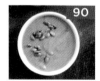 90
Sweet Potato Soup with Chipotle and Lime

CHAPTER 3:
HEARTY SOUPS

94
Spring Chicken Soup with Lemon and Asparagus

96
Harvest Chicken Soup with Sweet Potato Gnocchi

98
Sweet and Sour Cabbage Soup

100
Tom Yum

102
Tom Ka Gai (Thai Chicken Coconut Soup)

104
Classic Beef Pho

106
New England Clam Chowder

108
Manhattan Clam Chowder

110
Italian Wedding Soup

112
French Onion Soup

114
Minestrone with Orecchiette

116
Spicy Shrimp and Chorizo Soup

118
Meat and Potatoes Soup

120
Caldo Verde (Portuguese Potato Soup)

122
Hot and Sour Soup

124
Tuscan Tomato Soup

126
Matzo Ball Soup

128
Vietnamese Crab and Asparagus Soup

130
Egg Drop Soup

132
Build Your Own Ramen

134
Chicken Tortilla Soup

136
Chicken and Dumplings Soup

138
Beef Borscht

140
Burmese Chicken Noodle Soup

142
Lobster Bisque

144
Oxtail and Smoked Pork Gumbo with Spicy Roasted Okra

146
West African Cashew Soup

CHAPTER 4:
STEWS AND CHILIS

150

Five-Spice Beef Stew with Sweet Potatoes and Baby Bok Choy

152

Brazilian Fish Stew

154

San Francisco Cioppino

156

Orange and Olive Beef Stew

158

Spicy Lamb Curry

160

Pork and Apple Stew with Cabbage and Caraway

162

Zenbelly Chili 2.0

164

Roasted Tomatillo Pork Chili Verde

166

White Chicken Chili

168

Moroccan Vegetable Stew

CHAPTER 5:
CHILLED SOUPS

172

Green Gazpacho with Grapes and Almonds

174

Green Curry Avocado Soup

176

Grilled Vegetable Gazpacho with Lemon, Oregano, and Olives

178

Watermelon Gazpacho with Pistachios and Basil

180

Classic Gazpacho with Radishes and Chives

182

Summer Borscht with Cucumber and Dill

184

Chilled Carrot-Cumin Soup with Carrot Top–Cilantro Pesto

186

Spicy Peach Gazpacho

CHAPTER 6:
IN SOUP: Noodles & Other Fun Additions

190

Matzo Balls

192

Wontons

194

Veggie Noodles

196

Cauliflower Rice

198

Homemade Noodles or Orecchiette

200

Wrapper-Less Wontons

202

Sweet Potato Gnocchi

CHAPTER 7:
ON TOP: Garnishes to Add a Perfect Pop of Flavor & Texture

206
Pesto

208
Rosemary-Garlic Oil

210
Curry Coconut Cream

212
Croutons

214
Spiced Pepitas

216
Frizzled Leeks

218
Raita

220
Spiced Yogurt

CHAPTER 8:
ON THE SIDE: Breads, Crackers & Dippers

224
Breadsticks

226
Seeded Crackers

228
Garlic and Chive Crackers

230
Oyster Crackers

232
Flour Tortillas

234
Plantain Tortillas

236
Naan

238
Drop Biscuits

240
Jalapeño Cheddar Biscuits

242
Pull-Apart Dinner Rolls

244
Rye Bread

246
Baguettes

248
Mini Boules or Bread Bowls

250
Spicy Roasted Okra

CHAPTER 9:
SWEET SOUPS AND COOKIES

254
Crushed Strawberry Soup with Rose Shortbread Cookies

256
Orange Pistachio Soup with Raw Cacao Truffles

258
Summer Berry Soup with Chewy Ginger Cookies

260
Roasted Plum Soup with Cinnamon Roll Cookies

262
Chocolate Soup with Graham Cracker Marshmallow Dippers

GENERAL INDEX